A.A. Castor

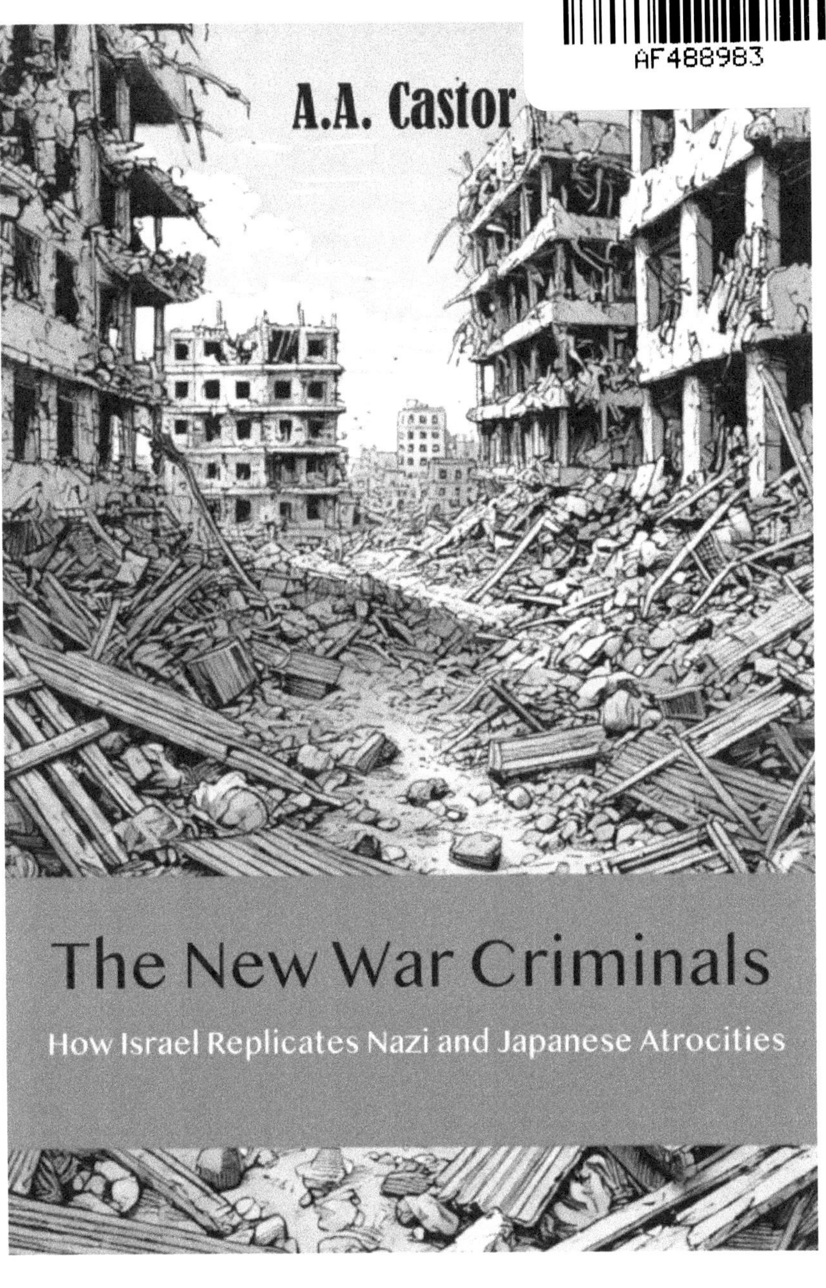

The New War Criminals

How Israel Replicates Nazi and Japanese Atrocities

Table of Contents

The New War Criminals: How Israel Replicates Nazi and Japanese Atrocities

A.A. Castor

Dedication

To my beloved family,

Your unconditional love, unwavering support, and endless encouragement have been my greatest blessings. From the earliest days of dreaming to the challenging moments of writing, you have stood by me with patience and belief. This book is as much yours as it is mine, a reflection of the values you've instilled and the faith you've shown in me. Thank you for being my rock and my inspiration.

To my dear friends,

Your friendship has illuminated my path with laughter, shared moments, and invaluable support. You've cheered me on through every triumph and lifted me up through every challenge. Your belief in my endeavors has been a source of strength and motivation. This book is a testament to the power of friendship, and I am grateful for each of you who has walked this journey by my side.

To God,

Your grace and guidance have been my constant companions. In moments of doubt, you've shown me the way; in moments of joy, you've multiplied my gratitude. This book is a testament to your faithfulness and the blessings you've bestowed upon me. May it serve as a reflection of your love and the lessons you continue to teach me.

With heartfelt gratitude and love,

A.A. Castor

Copyright © 2024 by A.A. Castor

All rights reserved. No part of this book may be reproduced, stored in a retrieval system, or transmitted in any form or by any means—electronic, mechanical, photocopy, recording, scanning, or otherwise—except as permitted under Section 107 or 108 of the 1976 United States Copyright Act, without the prior written permission of the publisher, except for brief quotations embodied in critical reviews and certain other noncommercial uses permitted by copyright law.

For permission requests, contact A.A. Castor at:

Address: Urban Deca Home Metro Manila, 1230

Email: dev.castortony@gmail.com

Website: www.tonyc.info[1]

This book is a work of non-fiction. Names, characters, places, and incidents are either the product of the author's research or are used factually. Any resemblance to actual persons, living or dead, events, or locales is entirely coincidental.

Printed in Philippines

Philippine Copyright Law:

The Intellectual Property Code of the Philippines (Republic Act No. 8293) provides protection to literary and artistic works from the moment of their creation. It includes provisions for the rights of authors and copyright owners, including the exclusive right to reproduce, distribute, perform, and display their works. Unauthorized use or reproduction of copyrighted materials is subject to legal penalties under this law.

---

1.   http://www.tonyc.info

Why I Am Writing This Book

As a **Filipino historian**, it is my responsibility to ensure that the lessons of history are not forgotten, especially as the **younger generation** seems to distance itself from the profound events of **World War II**. Many of the atrocities committed during that time—the **war crimes** of **Nazi Germany** and **Imperial Japan**—are fading from the collective memory of people my age and younger. What worries me even more is how they often overlook the fact that the actions of **Israel** today are the very things the world swore to never allow again. The **occupation**, the **displacement of people**, and the **dehumanization** of entire populations are the very patterns we said we would stop. Yet here we are, witnessing it happen again, and many remain indifferent or unaware.

As a **Filipino**, I feel this acutely, because my own people endured so much during **World War II** under the brutal occupation of **Imperial Japan**. The atrocities that took place in the Philippines—**massacres, forced labor**, and **the destruction of our cities**—left a deep scar on our national consciousness. The suffering endured by the Filipino people during the war was not just about the violence of battle, but about the systematic violation of human rights by an occupying power. The **Bataan Death March**, the **rape of our women**, the **forced displacement** of civilians—these are the horrors that we vowed never to allow again, not just for us, but for all nations.

But when I see what is happening in the **Palestinian territories**, I can't help but draw parallels to what my country experienced under Japanese rule. The **blockade of Gaza**, the destruction of homes, the

separation walls, and the **denial of basic rights** to Palestinians remind me of the suffering my ancestors endured under occupation. The world stood in solidarity with us then, as it did with all oppressed peoples after the war. The global community rallied around the idea that these crimes—whether against Filipinos, Jews, or any other group—must never happen again.

Yet, here we are today, and many have forgotten. It is my role as a historian to remind people of the past and to show them how these same patterns of **war crimes** and **human rights violations** are repeating today. Our collective memory is fragile, and if we do not protect it, the sacrifices of those who suffered will be in vain. The generation growing up now must understand that the atrocities of World War II are not just history—they are a warning. What is happening today in **Israel** and **Palestine** is what we fought against during the war, and it is what we must fight against now.

As Filipinos, we have a unique understanding of **occupation** and **oppression**, having lived through one of the most brutal experiences of the 20th century. It is our duty to stand in solidarity with those suffering similar fates today and to ensure that the world does not forget the promises made after World War II: that **no people** should have to endure the dehumanizing violence of **war crimes** and **illegal occupations**. Through history, we can understand the present, and through remembrance, we can ensure that justice and peace prevail for future generations.

Warning and Disclaimer

The author and publisher have made every effort to ensure the accuracy and reliability of the information presented in this book. However, the content is provided for **informational and educational purposes only** and should not be construed as legal, professional, or personal advice. The views and opinions expressed in this book are those of the author and do not necessarily reflect the official policy or position of any organization, institution, or entity.

No Liability: The author and publisher expressly disclaim any responsibility for errors, omissions, or interpretations of the material provided. The use of the information in this book is at the reader's own risk. The author and publisher are not liable for any losses, injuries, damages, or claims resulting from the application or interpretation of the information contained herein. This includes, but is not limited to, any direct, indirect, incidental, or consequential damages.

External Sources: Any references, links, or citations to external sources, websites, or documents are provided for informational purposes only. The author and publisher are not responsible for the accuracy, content, or availability of these external resources and do not endorse any third-party products or services mentioned within the book.

Sensitive Topics: This book may discuss controversial or sensitive topics. The author has approached these subjects with care and thorough research, but readers should be aware that the interpretation of historical events, legal issues, and geopolitical matters can vary.

Readers are encouraged to conduct their own independent research and consult professionals where appropriate.

No Guarantee of Outcomes: The author and publisher make no guarantees regarding the results or outcomes of applying the information contained in this book. Readers should be aware that historical, legal, and geopolitical situations are complex and multifaceted, and the material in this book is not intended to predict or guarantee any specific results.

About the Author

A.A. Castor is a **Filipino historian** with a deep passion for exploring the intersections of **history**, **leadership**, **politics**, and **social dynamics**. He is dedicated to uncovering the lessons of the past and applying them to modern challenges, offering readers practical insights and thought-provoking perspectives. With a focus on human rights, international law, and global conflicts, Castor's work spans a range of topics, from the moral and legal implications of historical war crimes to contemporary geopolitical issues.

As a historian, Castor draws on his extensive knowledge of **World War II** and its impact on nations, including the **Philippines**, to provide a unique understanding of **oppression**, **occupation**, and **resistance**. He connects these historical events to ongoing conflicts, such as the **Israeli-Palestinian conflict**, highlighting the repetition of atrocities the world once vowed never to allow again. His work seeks to remind readers that history holds valuable lessons about **justice**, **accountability**, and the **responsibility** of the global community to protect human rights.

In addition to his historical research, A.A. Castor has authored several books exploring political strategy, leadership principles, and the intricacies of **social governance**. His approach combines rigorous research with a strong narrative voice, aiming to engage readers while educating them on critical global issues.

A.A. Castor continues to write, podcast, and research on topics related to **leadership**, **history**, and **human rights**, always seeking to bridge the gap between the past and the present.

Chapter 1: A Legacy of Atrocities: Understanding the Parallels Between Israel's Actions and World War II War Crimes

In the annals of human history, there are events so brutal, so unthinkable, that they leave permanent scars on the collective conscience. The atrocities committed during World War II by Nazi Germany and Imperial Japan are among the darkest chapters of modern times. The genocides, forced displacements, bombings of civilians, and systematic efforts to erase entire cultures were war crimes that left a legacy of pain and devastation. These acts were condemned by the world, leading to international laws designed to ensure such horrors would never be repeated. Yet, despite the promises of "never again," history has a way of mirroring itself in disturbing ways.

In recent decades, the Israeli-Palestinian conflict has escalated to the point where many observers are drawing unsettling comparisons between the actions of Israel and those of Nazi Germany and Imperial Japan. From the collective punishment of civilian populations to the unlawful occupation of land, the echoes of the past reverberate with chilling familiarity. What makes this parallel so compelling is not just the nature of the violence but the methods employed: siege tactics, segregation, forced displacement, and cultural erasure—all bear stark resemblance to the tactics used by these regimes during WWII.

The purpose of this book is to explore these parallels in depth, not to draw simplistic or inflammatory conclusions, but to examine how the strategies and crimes of WWII continue to manifest in modern conflict. It is not merely a comparison for comparison's sake, but a necessary reflection on how the lessons of history are being ignored. By delving into these uncomfortable truths, we are forced to confront the reality that atrocities can, and do, repeat themselves. The global community's failure to hold Israel accountable for actions that mirror some of the worst offenses of the 20th century raises profound questions about international justice, human rights, and the selective application of accountability.

Israel's actions in Gaza and the West Bank—whether it be the indiscriminate bombing of civilian areas, the systematic destruction of Palestinian homes, or the creation of walls and barriers that enforce a modern-day apartheid—carry unmistakable echoes of the past. Just as Nazi Germany sought to reshape Europe through force and terror, and as Imperial Japan imposed its will on the people of East Asia, so too does Israel exert its control over the Palestinian territories. And, like the war criminals of WWII, these actions are often justified through a narrative of security and self-defense. Yet, the destruction wrought upon civilian populations, the dislocation of families, and the dismantling of cultural heritage reveal a deeper agenda: one of domination and control.

It is critical to examine these parallels not just to understand the ongoing conflict, but to prevent the further erosion of international norms that were established to prevent the recurrence of such crimes. The systematic nature of Israel's military strategies, its use of disproportionate force, and its settlement policies all fit the framework of crimes that should be universally condemned. Yet, due to political alliances and geopolitical interests, these actions have largely been shielded from the scrutiny that was so rigorously applied to Nazi Germany and Imperial Japan after the war.

This book seeks to challenge that silence. By drawing a direct line between the war crimes of the past and the actions of Israel today, it confronts the uncomfortable truth that history is, indeed, repeating itself. If the world continues to ignore these actions, it risks allowing the same kinds of atrocities that shaped the 20th century to define the 21st. This exploration is not just an academic exercise but a moral imperative. Understanding these parallels is essential to preventing future atrocities, ensuring justice, and holding power accountable in every era, whether it be in the 1940s or today.

A Dark Reflection: Israel's Actions and Their WWII Parallels

IN THE LANDSCAPE OF modern conflicts, few have garnered as much sustained global attention as the Israeli-Palestinian conflict. The struggle over land, identity, and sovereignty has been ongoing for decades, marked by military campaigns, ceasefires, and shattered peace accords. However, in recent years, a disturbing pattern has emerged, one that draws unsettling comparisons between Israel's actions in the Palestinian territories and the war crimes committed by Nazi Germany and Imperial Japan during World War II.

At the core of this comparison is the systematic use of force against civilian populations. In Nazi Germany, the persecution of Jews, Romani people, and other marginalized groups involved deliberate strategies of terror, ranging from the forced relocation of entire communities to the indiscriminate bombing of civilian areas. Similarly, Imperial Japan left a legacy of atrocities across Asia, where cities were leveled, civilians were massacred, and cultural identities were forcibly erased. These regimes operated under ideologies of racial superiority and national expansion, justifying their brutal methods as necessary for survival and dominance.

Today, Israel's actions in Gaza and the West Bank bear striking similarities to these tactics. The Israeli military's overwhelming response to acts of resistance—often in the form of bombings in densely populated areas—has led to thousands of civilian casualties. Hospitals, schools, and homes have been reduced to rubble, echoing the destruction wrought upon European and Asian cities during WWII. Like Nazi Germany's scorched-earth policies and Imperial Japan's relentless bombardments, Israel's military operations show little regard for the distinction between combatants and civilians, with widespread devastation inflicted on those simply trying to survive.

Another parallel lies in the use of collective punishment. Nazi Germany was infamous for punishing entire villages or towns for acts of resistance or defiance by a few individuals, with brutal consequences for those uninvolved. In Japan, civilians under occupation faced similar fates, with entire communities being subjected to punitive measures if suspected of harboring anti-Japanese sentiment. Israel's blockade of Gaza—severely restricting access to food, medicine, and essential resources—is a modern manifestation of this same philosophy. The blockade, coupled with regular military incursions, imposes unbearable suffering on an entire population, not because of individual actions, but because of their collective identity as Palestinians. This tactic has been condemned as a form of collective punishment, a clear violation of international law.

Perhaps most haunting is the forced displacement of populations, which mirrors the ethnic cleansing campaigns of WWII. Nazi Germany's expansion into Eastern Europe saw millions forcibly removed from their homes, with Jews and other marginalized groups sent to ghettos and concentration camps. Imperial Japan also displaced vast numbers of civilians as it expanded its empire, forcibly relocating people to consolidate control over territories. In the West Bank, Israeli settlements continue to expand, pushing Palestinians from their ancestral lands, demolishing homes, and building walls that carve up communities. These policies have led many to draw direct comparisons with the forcible removal of populations in WWII, where land was seized for the benefit of one group at the expense of another.

Cultural erasure is another key parallel. Just as Nazi Germany sought to wipe out Jewish culture through the destruction of synagogues, books, and historical landmarks, and Imperial Japan imposed its own culture on conquered territories, Israel's actions in the Palestinian territories have similarly targeted Palestinian identity. Ancient olive groves, cultural sites, and historical landmarks have been destroyed or confiscated, and Palestinian history is often rewritten or downplayed in Israeli narratives. The attempt to erase a people's history and identity is a tactic deeply rooted in the oppressive regimes of the past.

The comparison between Israel's current actions and the war crimes of WWII is not made lightly. The Holocaust and the atrocities committed by Imperial Japan remain among the darkest stains on human history. However, as time passes, the world must remain vigilant in recognizing the signs of history repeating itself. The strategies of occupation, control, and destruction that were used to such devastating effect in the 20th century are being echoed in the actions of a modern state against an occupied people.

In drawing these comparisons, the goal is not to diminish the horrors of WWII, but to emphasize the universal lessons that should have been learned from them. War crimes, regardless of when or where they occur, must be recognized, condemned, and stopped. Failing to do so allows the patterns of violence, oppression, and dehumanization to continue into new eras, affecting new generations, and perpetuating the cycle of suffering.

Learning from the Past: Why the Israel-WWII Comparison Matters Today

THE COMPARISON BETWEEN Israel's actions in the Palestinian territories and the war crimes committed by Nazi Germany and Imperial Japan might seem harsh, but it is an essential lens through which to view modern conflict. In examining this parallel, the true purpose of the comparison becomes clear: to learn from the past and prevent future atrocities. History has a way of repeating itself when its darkest moments are not properly scrutinized, and the failure to recognize the signs of emerging patterns of oppression can lead to disastrous consequences.

After the horrors of World War II, the international community vowed to never let such crimes happen again. The Nuremberg and Tokyo Trials brought justice to the perpetrators, and global institutions like the United Nations were established with the express purpose of safeguarding human rights and preventing large-scale atrocities. Yet, despite these safeguards, we find ourselves today observing situations that disturbingly resemble the very actions these institutions were created to stop.

The actions of Israel, particularly in Gaza and the West Bank, serve as a modern reflection of the methods used by past regimes to justify violence, control populations, and expand territory. This is why the comparison is so vital. It forces us to confront uncomfortable truths: that the mechanisms of power and control used by Nazi Germany and Imperial Japan are still relevant today, only adapted to new circumstances and new actors. These methods—collective punishment, targeting civilians, forced displacement, and cultural erasure—were not born out of a vacuum in the 20th century, nor did they disappear when the regimes that employed them were defeated. They are part of a larger human tendency toward domination and violence that reemerges when left unchecked.

This comparison is not just about condemning Israel's actions, but about understanding the universal patterns of conflict and oppression that have persisted through history. By examining these parallels, we are better equipped to identify the early warning signs of atrocity and to intervene before it escalates. Recognizing that modern actions echo past crimes is the first step in preventing them from reaching the same scale of devastation.

Moreover, the necessity of examining these parallels lies in the failure of international accountability. After World War II, war crimes were treated with the utmost seriousness, leading to landmark trials that set the standard for how the world should respond to such violations. Today, however, Israel operates with a degree of impunity. Political alliances, strategic interests, and global power dynamics often shield Israel from the consequences of its actions, allowing the situation in the Palestinian territories to worsen. The lack of meaningful accountability for war crimes and human rights violations in this context weakens the global commitment to human rights and emboldens other states to act with similar disregard for international law.

The repetition of history also underscores the dangers of ignoring the lessons learned from past atrocities. After WWII, the world said "never again," yet genocides and war crimes have continued in places like Rwanda, Bosnia, Syria, and now, in the ongoing Israeli-Palestinian conflict. Each time, the international community has been slow to act, and each time, the results have been devastating. By drawing a clear line between Israel's actions and those of Nazi Germany and Imperial Japan, this book serves as a reminder of the consequences of inaction and the price of allowing history to repeat itself.

In the end, the necessity of examining these parallels is about more than just historical reflection; it is about creating a more just and peaceful future. If we fail to recognize the repetition of these patterns of violence and oppression, we doom ourselves to perpetuating them. By understanding how Israel's actions reflect the tactics of past war criminals, we open the door to a broader conversation about justice, human rights, and the importance of holding all nations accountable for their actions—regardless of their political power or global standing.

This book aims to be a clarion call, urging the world to pay attention before it is too late. If we do not confront the uncomfortable parallels between past and present, we risk allowing atrocities to continue unchecked, with devastating consequences for future generations. History repeats itself, but it does not have to—if we are willing to learn from its lessons.

Chapter 2: The Shadows of the Past: Nazi Germany and Imperial Japan's War Crimes

World War II stands as one of the most cataclysmic periods in human history, marked by unfathomable violence, mass suffering, and some of the most heinous crimes ever committed. The brutality unleashed by Nazi Germany and Imperial Japan was not limited to the battlefields but extended to the civilian populations they sought to dominate, control, and eliminate. Their actions left deep scars on the global psyche and forever changed the way the world views war, humanity, and justice. These atrocities were not simply tragic byproducts of conflict; they were deliberate, calculated efforts to annihilate entire populations, seize territory, and impose dominance. The consequences of their crimes reverberate to this day, shaping international law, human rights norms, and the world's commitment to preventing future atrocities.

Nazi Germany's war crimes are among the most widely studied and condemned in history. The regime's systematic persecution of Jews during the Holocaust stands as the most notorious of these crimes. Six million Jews were exterminated in concentration camps, gas chambers, and death marches, driven by a genocidal ideology that sought to eradicate an entire people. But the horrors of the Nazi regime extended beyond the Holocaust. In occupied territories across Europe, entire cities were subjected to collective punishment for acts of resistance or defiance. The Jewish ghettos, such as those in Warsaw, were overcrowded, under-resourced, and designed to trap civilians in desperate conditions. Forced displacement, whether through the relocation of civilians to camps or the resettlement of Germans in newly conquered lands, was another hallmark of Nazi expansion. Civilians were not just collateral damage; they were the targets of Nazi cruelty.

Imperial Japan's crimes, though sometimes overshadowed by the scale of the Holocaust, were no less brutal. The Nanjing Massacre, one of the most infamous atrocities of WWII, saw Japanese troops slaughter hundreds of thousands of Chinese civilians in a six-week campaign of terror. Beyond the massacre, forced labor camps were a staple of Japan's war efforts, with millions of civilians and prisoners of war subjected to grueling, often fatal conditions. Bombings of civilian targets across China, the Philippines, and Korea spread destruction far beyond the immediate battle zones. Japan's conquest was also marked by an aggressive campaign of cultural erasure, where local languages, customs, and histories were suppressed in favor of Japanese culture and control. The scars of this cultural destruction still linger in the collective memory of these nations.

These atrocities, committed on a scale previously unimaginable, forced the world to confront the question of how to hold accountable those responsible for such inhumanity. In the aftermath of WWII, the Nuremberg Trials for Nazi war criminals and the Tokyo Trials for Japanese leaders set a new precedent in international law, establishing the principle that individuals, including state leaders, could be held criminally responsible for war crimes, genocide, and crimes against humanity. These trials were groundbreaking in their scope and served as the foundation for the creation of international laws that govern war crimes and human rights violations today. The horrors of Nazi Germany and Imperial Japan gave birth to the Geneva Conventions, which sought to protect civilians, prisoners of war, and combatants in future conflicts.

The lessons learned from these war crimes are embedded in the global consciousness, serving as a stark reminder of the depths to which humanity can sink when driven by hatred, expansionist ambitions, and unchecked power. Yet, despite the international legal frameworks that emerged from these dark chapters, the repetition of similar tactics in modern conflicts, such as those seen in Israel's treatment of Palestinians, forces us to ask: Have we truly learned from the past? Or are we simply allowing history to repeat itself under a new guise?

By exploring the atrocities committed by Nazi Germany and Imperial Japan, it becomes clear that the methods of collective punishment, forced displacement, targeting of civilians, and cultural erasure are not relics of history. They are strategies of domination that resurface time and again when one group seeks to subjugate another. The global community's response to these atrocities during WWII set the stage for how we understand and judge war crimes today. But as these tactics emerge in new conflicts, the world is reminded that the fight for justice and humanity is never truly over. The same mechanisms of oppression, if left unchecked, can continue to plague the world, creating new victims and perpetuating cycles of violence.

The Dark Legacy of Nazi Germany's War Crimes

NAZI GERMANY'S ATROCITIES during World War II represent one of the most horrific chapters in human history, defined by genocide, systemic violence, and a deliberate campaign to annihilate millions of people. Central to these atrocities was the Holocaust, the Nazi regime's systematic extermination of six million Jews across Europe. But while the Holocaust remains the most well-known crime of the Third Reich, it was part of a broader pattern of brutality that targeted not only Jews but also Romani people, disabled individuals, political dissidents, and ethnic minorities, along with entire civilian populations in occupied territories.

The Nazi war machine was driven by an ideology of racial superiority, viewing certain groups as subhuman and unworthy of life. This led to the creation of ghettos, where Jews and other undesirables were forcibly relocated and confined in appalling conditions. Ghettos, such as the infamous Warsaw Ghetto, were overcrowded, disease-ridden, and deliberately cut off from essential supplies like food and medicine. Families were torn apart, and those who survived did so under constant threat of deportation to concentration or death camps. The ghettos were not just holding areas—they were designed as a tool of slow extermination through starvation and neglect, a chilling precursor to the death camps that followed.

One of the most terrifying aspects of Nazi Germany's rule was its use of collective punishment. Whenever resistance movements emerged in occupied countries, the Nazis responded with brutal reprisals. Entire towns and villages were massacred or razed to the ground in retaliation for the actions of a few. In places like Lidice in Czechoslovakia, a single act of resistance could lead to the execution of all men, the deportation of women and children, and the total destruction of the village. These acts were meant to instill fear in the occupied populations, discouraging rebellion and solidifying Nazi control through terror.

Forced displacement was another hallmark of Nazi atrocities. As the German army advanced across Europe, millions of civilians were uprooted from their homes. The Nazis' quest for *Lebensraum*—living space—meant that entire populations were forcibly removed to make way for German settlers. In Eastern Europe, this resulted in the displacement of millions of Poles, Ukrainians, and other Slavic peoples, whom the Nazis viewed as inferior. Those deemed racially unfit or politically undesirable were deported to concentration camps, where they faced starvation, forced labor, and, often, death. The Nazi policy of ethnic cleansing extended beyond physical displacement, as entire cultures were erased through the destruction of religious sites, libraries, and cultural landmarks.

The targeting of civilians was not just a byproduct of Nazi military campaigns but a deliberate strategy. Civilians in occupied territories were subjected to aerial bombings, mass shootings, and orchestrated campaigns of terror. The Nazi occupation of the Soviet Union, for example, was characterized by the mass execution of civilians, especially in areas where the local population was suspected of aiding resistance fighters. Einsatzgruppen, mobile killing units, followed the German army's advance, rounding up and executing Jews, intellectuals, communists, and anyone perceived as a threat to Nazi authority. These executions were carried out with methodical efficiency, often in broad daylight, and were part of a larger effort to exterminate all potential sources of opposition to Nazi rule.

The culmination of these atrocities was the industrial-scale extermination carried out in concentration and death camps such as Auschwitz, Treblinka, and Sobibor. These camps were not merely places of detention; they were specifically designed to kill as many people as possible in the shortest amount of time. Prisoners were subjected to inhumane conditions, forced labor, and medical experiments. The use of gas chambers, where thousands of men, women, and children were murdered daily, represents the ultimate expression of Nazi cruelty. The systematic nature of the Holocaust, with its trains, camps, and gas chambers, was unprecedented in history—a cold, calculated machine of death.

The sheer scale and horror of Nazi Germany's war crimes left an indelible mark on the world. These crimes were not just acts of war; they were acts of annihilation, fueled by a perverse ideology that sought to remake the world according to a twisted racial hierarchy. The lessons of the Holocaust and other atrocities committed by the Nazis continue to shape the global understanding of genocide, human rights, and war crimes, reminding the world of the depths to which humanity can sink when hatred and violence go unchecked.

Imperial Japan's War Crimes: A Legacy of Brutality and Destruction

DURING WORLD WAR II, Imperial Japan's military expansion across Asia was accompanied by a wave of atrocities that left deep scars on the countries it occupied. Driven by the ambition to dominate Asia and assert its supremacy, Japan engaged in a series of war crimes that mirrored the ruthless campaigns of Nazi Germany in Europe. These atrocities, marked by mass killings, forced labor, and cultural erasure, have left a lasting legacy of pain and devastation in the regions Japan sought to conquer.

One of the most infamous war crimes committed by Imperial Japan was the **Nanjing Massacre**. In December 1937, Japanese forces captured the Chinese city of Nanjing, and what followed was a six-week orgy of violence and terror that shocked the world. Japanese soldiers systematically raped, murdered, and tortured the civilian population. An estimated 200,000 to 300,000 people were killed, including women, children, and the elderly. The brutality was staggering—victims were shot, beheaded, burned alive, or used for bayonet practice. Women were subjected to mass rape, often followed by their murder. This was not random violence but an orchestrated campaign of terror designed to break the spirit of the Chinese people and assert Japanese dominance.

Beyond the horrors of Nanjing, Imperial Japan's crimes extended to the forced labor of millions of civilians and prisoners of war. Throughout its occupied territories in China, Korea, the Philippines, and Southeast Asia, Japan conscripted men, women, and children into labor camps under brutal conditions. These laborers were forced to work in mines, factories, and infrastructure projects, such as the infamous Burma-Thailand railway, often referred to as the "Death Railway." Those who survived the backbreaking labor faced starvation, disease, and physical abuse at the hands of their captors. The mortality rate in these camps was extraordinarily high, with thousands of forced laborers dying from malnutrition, exhaustion, and cruel treatment. Korean women, known as "comfort women," were particularly victimized, being forced into sexual slavery for Japanese soldiers—a war crime that continues to fuel tensions in East Asia to this day.

Japan's military campaign was not limited to the battlefield but deliberately targeted civilians through widespread bombing raids across the region. Entire cities were flattened, and civilian infrastructure was obliterated. Japanese forces bombed Chinese cities, including Chongqing, with little regard for the civilian population, resulting in the deaths of tens of thousands of non-combatants. These bombings were part of a broader strategy to weaken the resolve of the Chinese people by inflicting terror on the population. In Southeast Asia, the Philippines, and other territories, civilians were often caught in the crossfire of Japanese military campaigns, with villages and towns reduced to rubble in the pursuit of imperial control.

In addition to the physical destruction of life and property, Imperial Japan engaged in a deliberate campaign of **cultural erasure** in the territories it occupied. In Korea, Japan sought to eliminate Korean identity by banning the use of the Korean language in schools, replacing Korean names with Japanese ones, and imposing Japanese culture and traditions on the population. Temples, historical sites, and cultural artifacts were destroyed or co-opted as symbols of Japanese rule. Similar efforts were made in Taiwan and Manchuria, where local languages and customs were suppressed to assimilate these regions into the Japanese empire. The goal was clear: to obliterate the cultural heritage of the occupied peoples and replace it with a homogeneous Japanese identity that would serve the empire's ambitions.

Imperial Japan's war crimes were not isolated incidents but part of a broader strategy of domination through terror, forced submission, and cultural annihilation. The legacy of these crimes still haunts the countries affected, with survivors and their descendants bearing the scars—both physical and psychological—of Japan's brutal occupation. These atrocities have shaped international law and justice in the post-war era, particularly in the prosecution of war crimes and crimes against humanity at the Tokyo Trials. Yet, much like Germany's Holocaust, Japan's actions during WWII stand as a sobering reminder of how unchecked power, expansionist ambitions, and racial superiority can lead to unimaginable suffering.

The Lasting Impact of WWII Crimes on International Law and Global Justice

THE ATROCITIES COMMITTED during World War II by Nazi Germany and Imperial Japan were unprecedented in their scale and brutality, shaking the foundations of human civilization. The sheer magnitude of these crimes—genocide, forced labor, mass bombings, and systematic campaigns of ethnic cleansing—led to a global reckoning with the horrors of war. In the aftermath of the conflict, the world was forced to confront not only the consequences of these acts but also the failure of existing legal frameworks to prevent such atrocities. This realization drove the development of new international laws and institutions that would reshape the way war crimes and crimes against humanity are understood and prosecuted.

One of the most significant outcomes of WWII was the establishment of the **Nuremberg Trials**, where the leaders of Nazi Germany were held accountable for their roles in orchestrating the Holocaust and other war crimes. For the first time in history, the international community convened to prosecute individuals, not only for crimes committed during warfare but also for the systemic extermination of entire populations. The Nuremberg Trials set an important precedent: that individuals, regardless of their rank or position, could be held criminally responsible for war crimes, genocide, and crimes against humanity. This was a profound shift in international law, which had previously focused primarily on state responsibility rather than individual culpability.

In parallel, the **Tokyo Trials** sought to bring justice to the leaders of Imperial Japan, who were responsible for crimes ranging from the Nanjing Massacre to the forced labor of millions of civilians across Asia. These trials were pivotal in defining the legal concept of war crimes and human rights violations. They introduced the idea that military leaders and government officials could not hide behind the excuse of following orders. "Crimes against humanity" became a formal legal term, encompassing a broad range of atrocities, including mass murder, enslavement, and the persecution of entire groups of people.

The legacy of these trials is profound. They laid the groundwork for the **Geneva Conventions**, a series of international treaties that aimed to protect the rights of civilians, prisoners of war, and combatants during times of conflict. The Geneva Conventions established clear legal standards for the humane treatment of individuals during war, prohibiting acts such as torture, inhumane treatment, and collective punishment. These principles have become the cornerstone of international humanitarian law, providing a legal framework for the conduct of war and the protection of human rights.

World War II also had a lasting impact on the **global consciousness** regarding the moral and legal obligations of states and individuals. The widespread documentation of Nazi and Japanese war crimes brought the realities of genocide and mass atrocities into sharp focus. The Holocaust, in particular, became a symbol of the dangers of unchecked hatred, racism, and authoritarianism. The phrase "never again" became a rallying cry for those determined to prevent future genocides, and the world recognized the need for stronger mechanisms to protect vulnerable populations.

This led to the creation of institutions like the **United Nations**, which was founded in 1945 with the explicit goal of promoting peace, security, and human rights. The UN's **Universal Declaration of Human Rights** (1948) was a direct response to the horrors of WWII, affirming the dignity and rights of every human being, regardless of nationality, ethnicity, or religion. The Declaration set the stage for the modern human rights movement, emphasizing that atrocities like those committed during the war were not merely violations of wartime conduct but violations of the fundamental principles of human dignity.

The crimes of WWII also spurred the development of the **International Criminal Court (ICC)**, which was established in 2002 to prosecute individuals for war crimes, genocide, and crimes against humanity. The ICC builds on the legacy of the Nuremberg and Tokyo Trials, creating a permanent international institution dedicated to bringing justice to those responsible for the most egregious violations of international law. While the ICC faces challenges, including political resistance and limitations on its jurisdiction, it represents a significant step forward in the global fight against impunity for war crimes.

The impact of WWII war crimes continues to shape international law and justice. The principles established in the wake of these atrocities have been invoked in subsequent conflicts, from the Balkans to Rwanda and beyond. The global community has become more aware of the warning signs of genocide and mass violence, leading to interventions in some cases and efforts to hold perpetrators accountable in others. The term "war crimes" now carries with it the weight of history, a reminder of the devastating consequences of allowing such actions to go unchecked.

Yet, despite these advancements, the recurrence of atrocities in various parts of the world—whether through ethnic cleansing, forced displacement, or civilian bombings—shows that the lessons of WWII must constantly be reinforced. The laws and institutions established in response to these crimes are not infallible, and the global community must remain vigilant in enforcing them. The legacy of Nazi Germany and Imperial Japan is not just one of horror but of the ongoing struggle to ensure that the atrocities of the past are never repeated. The systems of international law and justice that emerged from WWII are a testament to humanity's commitment to a better future, but they also serve as a reminder of the fragility of peace and the importance of accountability in preserving it.

Chapter 3: Collective Punishment and Siege Tactics: From WWII to Modern Conflicts

One of the most insidious strategies used in wartime is the deliberate punishment of civilian populations for the actions of a few. During World War II, both Nazi Germany and Imperial Japan engaged in collective punishment and siege tactics as a means to terrorize, subjugate, and demoralize their enemies. These brutal strategies were not aimed solely at military forces, but at entire communities, turning ordinary civilians into targets. The intent was clear: by punishing the many for the actions of a few, these regimes hoped to break the spirit of resistance and crush any opposition through fear, deprivation, and death. In modern times, similar strategies have been employed in the Israeli-Palestinian conflict, particularly through Israel's blockade of Gaza, which has drawn stark parallels to the siege tactics of WWII.

Nazi Germany was notorious for its use of **collective punishment** in the territories it occupied. Whenever resistance fighters, partisans, or even individuals opposed Nazi rule, the German military responded with brutal reprisals against entire communities. In places like Lidice in Czechoslovakia, the assassination of a high-ranking Nazi official led to the village being wiped off the map. All men were executed, women and children were deported to concentration camps, and the village was burned to the ground. This was not an isolated event—across occupied Europe, similar acts of retaliation were carried out. The Nazis believed that by making an example of these communities, they could suppress any further resistance. The message was clear: any act of defiance, no matter how small, would result in the indiscriminate suffering of innocent civilians. Collective punishment became a tool of terror, creating a culture of fear where people were forced to choose between resisting oppression or ensuring the survival of their families and communities.

Imperial Japan also employed **siege and starvation tactics** as a central part of its strategy to subdue civilian populations and break the will of its enemies. In the siege of Changsha and other Chinese cities, Japanese forces deliberately cut off access to food, medicine, and essential supplies, forcing civilians to endure starvation and disease. These sieges were not just about defeating an enemy army; they were about punishing and weakening the civilian population to hasten surrender. By denying civilians the basic necessities of life, Japan hoped to cripple morale and eliminate any possibility of resistance. Entire communities were left to starve, with the Japanese military showing little regard for human life. These siege tactics were not only a means of military conquest but also a way to assert dominance over the occupied territories, demonstrating the extent of Imperial Japan's ruthlessness.

Fast forward to the present day, and **Israel's blockade of Gaza** bears striking similarities to these WWII tactics. Since 2007, Gaza has been under a land, air, and sea blockade imposed by Israel, severely limiting the movement of goods, people, and essential supplies. The blockade has led to widespread shortages of food, medicine, and fuel, plunging Gaza into a humanitarian crisis. Like the sieges employed by Nazi Germany and Imperial Japan, the blockade of Gaza punishes an entire population for the actions of a few. Israel argues that the blockade is necessary to prevent weapons smuggling and protect its citizens from Hamas attacks, but the impact on Gaza's civilian population has been devastating. The blockade has crippled the local economy, caused widespread poverty, and left the healthcare system on the brink of collapse.

In addition to the blockade, **airstrikes** targeting infrastructure in Gaza have further exacerbated the suffering of civilians. Water treatment facilities, power plants, and hospitals have been bombed, leaving thousands without access to clean water, electricity, or medical care. The denial of these basic necessities mirrors the tactics of Nazi and Japanese forces, where civilian populations were deliberately targeted to weaken the enemy's resolve. Israel's military operations in Gaza, while framed as self-defense, often result in disproportionate harm to civilians, with entire neighborhoods reduced to rubble in response to rocket fire from militant groups.

The parallels between these tactics are undeniable. In all three cases—Nazi Germany, Imperial Japan, and modern-day Israel—the use of collective punishment and siege tactics was justified as necessary for security or military objectives. Yet, the result is always the same: the innocent bear the brunt of the suffering. Civilians are trapped in a cycle of fear, deprivation, and violence, with little hope of reprieve. These strategies, rooted in the belief that breaking the spirit of the people will bring about victory, only serve to deepen resentment, fuel anger, and prolong the conflict.

The lessons of history are clear. Collective punishment and siege tactics do not bring about lasting peace or security. Instead, they perpetuate cycles of violence and suffering, creating generations of people scarred by the trauma of war. Whether in WWII or today, the deliberate targeting of civilian populations is a violation of international law and a stain on the moral conscience of the global community. Yet, these tactics continue to be used, a grim reminder that the darkest strategies of the past are still with us today, adapted to new conflicts and new enemies.

Nazi Germany's Collective Punishment: Terrorizing Civilian Populations in Occupied Territories

DURING ITS OCCUPATION of much of Europe, Nazi Germany employed a brutal strategy of collective punishment against civilian populations, aiming to crush resistance and maintain its grip on conquered territories. Collective punishment, as practiced by the Nazis, was the deliberate infliction of suffering on entire communities in response to the actions of a few. Resistance movements, sabotage, or any form of defiance against Nazi rule were met with disproportionate retaliation, not only against those responsible but also against civilians who had no involvement in the resistance. This tactic was designed to instill terror, suppress any future attempts at rebellion, and demonstrate the ruthless efficiency of the Nazi regime.

One of the most notorious examples of Nazi collective punishment took place in **Lidice**, a small village in Czechoslovakia. After the assassination of Reinhard Heydrich, a high-ranking Nazi official and one of the architects of the Holocaust, Hitler ordered immediate reprisals. Even though the assassins had no direct connection to the village, the entire male population of Lidice—173 men—was executed. Women and children were either sent to concentration camps or, in the case of some children, sent to be "Germanized." The village itself was burned to the ground, and any remaining buildings were razed to erase its existence. This act of collective punishment sent a chilling message to other occupied nations: resistance would result in the annihilation of entire communities.

The use of collective punishment was not limited to major incidents like the one in Lidice. Throughout occupied Europe, particularly in Eastern Europe and the Balkans, Nazi forces routinely executed civilians in reprisal for acts of resistance or sabotage. In **Poland**, where resistance was widespread, Nazi troops regularly carried out mass executions of civilians as retribution for attacks on German soldiers. In one such instance, following the assassination of German soldiers in Warsaw, hundreds of Poles were rounded up and executed in retaliation. The Nazis believed that by making an example of these communities, they could deter future resistance. Civilians lived in constant fear that any act of defiance—whether by partisans, underground fighters, or even a single individual—could bring deadly consequences upon their entire town or village.

In **France**, the massacre of **Oradour-sur-Glane** stands as another horrific example of Nazi collective punishment. In June 1944, following the D-Day landings, French resistance forces intensified their attacks on German occupiers. In response, an SS Panzer division entered the village of Oradour-sur-Glane and, without warning, massacred 642 residents. Men were gathered in barns and machine-gunned, while women and children were locked inside a church that was then set on fire. The village was looted and destroyed, left as a smoldering ruin. This atrocity was intended to serve as a deterrent to further resistance, demonstrating that any perceived threat to German rule would be met with swift and overwhelming violence.

Nazi collective punishment also extended to the use of **concentration camps**, where entire populations were deported and subjected to inhumane conditions as punishment for acts of resistance or simply for being part of an ethnic group deemed undesirable by the regime. In **Belarus**, where partisans waged a fierce resistance campaign against the Germans, entire villages were depopulated and sent to camps as collective punishment. The Nazi regime viewed these populations as not only a threat but as expendable, using mass deportation and imprisonment to assert control.

The tactic of collective punishment was deeply rooted in the Nazis' ideology of racial superiority and their belief that entire groups—whether defined by ethnicity, religion, or political affiliation—were collectively responsible for any actions that undermined German rule. This concept of collective guilt was a key aspect of the regime's racial policies, where entire populations were held accountable for the actions of a few. The result was widespread terror, as civilians had no control over whether their community might become the next target of Nazi retribution.

Beyond its immediate impact of instilling fear and breaking the will of civilian populations, collective punishment had long-term consequences. It fostered a climate of distrust and paranoia, as people became wary of associating with resistance movements out of fear that they would bring destruction upon their families and neighbors. Entire regions were depopulated, villages wiped off the map, and cultural landmarks destroyed, all in the name of Nazi domination.

Nazi Germany's use of collective punishment in occupied territories was a clear violation of international law, even by the standards of the time. The Geneva Conventions, although not fully developed in their modern form during WWII, explicitly prohibited such reprisals against civilians. Yet, the Nazi regime, driven by its racist and militaristic ideology, showed little regard for these laws. Instead, it weaponized collective punishment as a tool of oppression, sending shockwaves of terror throughout Europe and leaving a legacy of atrocity that continues to haunt the memories of the affected nations.

The legacy of these tactics underscores the importance of international law in protecting civilians during wartime. The sheer brutality of Nazi collective punishment practices served as a catalyst for the development of post-war legal frameworks aimed at preventing such atrocities. The crimes committed by Nazi forces in occupied territories were later prosecuted at the Nuremberg Trials, where key officials were held accountable for their roles in directing and carrying out these acts of terror. Today, the principles established in response to these war crimes serve as a reminder of the need to safeguard the rights of civilians in conflict zones and to hold accountable those who violate them.

Imperial Japan's Siege and Starvation Tactics: Deliberately Targeting Civilians to Break the Enemy

THROUGHOUT WORLD WAR II, Imperial Japan employed siege and starvation tactics as part of its brutal strategy to subdue both enemy forces and civilian populations across Asia. These tactics were not just about military conquest but about systematically breaking the will of entire communities by cutting off their access to food, water, and essential supplies. By turning civilians into direct targets, Japan aimed to weaken the resolve of its enemies, creating widespread suffering as a means to force surrender. These deliberate acts of starvation and siege were among the many war crimes committed by Imperial Japan, leaving a legacy of devastation in the territories it occupied.

One of the most notorious examples of Japan's siege tactics occurred during the prolonged **Battle of Changsha** in China. For years, Japanese forces attempted to capture the strategically important city, but when their initial military assaults failed, they resorted to surrounding the city and cutting off supplies. The siege of Changsha was characterized by the Japanese army's deliberate strategy to isolate the city, preventing food, medicine, and any aid from reaching the civilian population. The goal was to starve the city into submission, weakening the morale of both the defenders and the people. As food supplies dwindled, hunger and disease spread rapidly, and the once-thriving city was reduced to desperation. This tactic, employed repeatedly in China, demonstrated Japan's willingness to use civilians as pawns in their larger military campaigns, indifferent to the humanitarian toll of such actions.

Japan's siege strategy was not limited to direct blockades. In many cases, the Japanese military conducted **scorched-earth campaigns** as they advanced through enemy territory, destroying crops, water supplies, and infrastructure that civilians depended on for survival.

This left entire regions unable to support their populations, leading to widespread starvation and displacement. For instance, in the Chinese countryside, where much of the resistance against Japanese occupation was concentrated, the Japanese army burned villages, destroyed farmlands, and poisoned water sources to ensure that both combatants and non-combatants would suffer. The deliberate destruction of resources vital to civilian survival was a cruel tactic designed to weaken any resistance by targeting the population's ability to sustain itself.

Another horrific example of Japan's starvation tactics occurred during the **occupation of the Philippines**. As Japanese forces faced increasing resistance from Filipino guerillas and the American military, they turned to punitive measures that included widespread starvation of civilians. In **Manila**, Japan imposed strict food rationing and diverted much-needed supplies to the military, leaving civilians to fend for themselves in a city devastated by bombings and sieges. Japanese forces systematically destroyed food stocks and cut off supply lines, ensuring that civilians suffered the most. Starvation spread rapidly, and disease followed closely behind as sanitation systems collapsed. The people of Manila, already trapped in a city under siege, endured horrific conditions as the Japanese army sought to maintain its grip on the city by inflicting as much suffering on civilians as possible.

The use of starvation as a weapon extended beyond the battlefield and into Japan's notorious **labor camps** across its occupied territories. Civilians and prisoners of war were often subjected to forced labor under brutal conditions, with minimal food and water provided. Many were starved to death as they toiled in mines, railways, and other infrastructure projects. One of the most infamous examples is the construction of the **Burma-Thailand Railway**, often referred to as the "Death Railway." The Japanese forced tens of thousands of Allied prisoners of war and local civilians to work in harsh conditions with little to no food. The mortality rate was staggering, as workers succumbed to starvation, disease, and exhaustion. For the Japanese military, the lives of these civilians and prisoners were expendable, and starvation was just another tool to exert control and maximize labor output.

Throughout its empire, Japan's occupation was marked by the systematic **looting and confiscation of food resources**. In **Korea, Manchuria**, and **Southeast Asia**, Japanese forces requisitioned rice, livestock, and other essential supplies, often leaving the local population on the brink of famine. The resources were diverted to feed Japan's military machine, while the civilians under its rule were left to starve. In some cases, Japanese authorities even set price controls that made it impossible for locals to afford what little food was available. This deliberate economic warfare was another form of starvation tactic, ensuring that the populations in these territories would suffer from hunger and malnutrition while Japan reaped the benefits of their resources.

Japan's **naval blockades** further amplified the suffering. In places like the **Dutch East Indies** (modern-day Indonesia), Japan's control of sea routes made it nearly impossible for vital supplies to reach the civilian population. With food imports halted and local resources drained by the occupying forces, starvation became rampant. As in other territories, the Japanese military made little distinction between combatants and civilians, treating the deprivation of essential goods as an acceptable strategy to ensure domination over the region.

The widespread use of starvation and siege tactics by Imperial Japan was not only a means of breaking enemy morale but also a tool for asserting its dominance and extracting resources from the populations it occupied. Civilians became collateral damage in Japan's pursuit of military victory and imperial expansion. These tactics, which deliberately targeted non-combatants, were clear violations of the laws of war even by the standards of the time. They demonstrated a blatant disregard for human life and dignity, contributing to the immense suffering endured by millions of people across Asia.

The impact of these war crimes continued long after the war ended. Survivors of Japanese sieges and starvation tactics bore the physical and psychological scars of prolonged deprivation, with many communities struggling to rebuild in the face of widespread famine and economic collapse. The Tokyo Trials sought to bring some accountability to Japan's wartime leadership, but the legacy of these crimes still haunts the memories of the affected populations. Imperial Japan's siege and starvation tactics remain a stark reminder of the lengths to which authoritarian regimes will go to assert control, with civilians often paying the highest price.

Israel's Blockade of Gaza: Modern Siege Tactics and the Denial of Basic Human Rights

IN THE ONGOING ISRAELI-Palestinian conflict, the blockade of Gaza has become a glaring example of modern siege tactics that bear striking similarities to those employed by Nazi Germany and Imperial Japan during World War II. Since 2007, Israel has imposed a strict blockade on Gaza, restricting the movement of people and goods by land, sea, and air. The blockade has crippled Gaza's economy, led to widespread shortages of essential supplies, and trapped the population in what has been described by many human rights organizations as an "open-air prison." This deliberate strategy of deprivation and isolation closely mirrors the siege and starvation tactics used in WWII to weaken civilian populations and force submission.

The **blockade of Gaza** has severely restricted the import of food, medicine, fuel, and construction materials, leaving the population in a constant state of crisis. While Israel justifies the blockade as a necessary measure to prevent weapons smuggling and protect its citizens from Hamas, the impact on the civilian population has been devastating. Gaza's residents face chronic shortages of clean water, electricity, and medical supplies, with hospitals unable to treat the wounded or provide adequate care for the sick. The blockade's stranglehold on essential goods creates a humanitarian disaster, where civilians are punished en masse for the actions of a few. This collective punishment echoes the policies of Nazi Germany in occupied territories, where entire communities were subjected to deprivation as a form of retaliation or control.

Beyond the physical blockade, **airstrikes** on Gaza have compounded the suffering of civilians. Israeli airstrikes, often in response to rocket attacks by militant groups, have resulted in widespread destruction of civilian infrastructure. Hospitals, schools, power plants, and water treatment facilities have been repeatedly targeted or damaged in these strikes, leaving the population without access to basic services. Much like the indiscriminate bombings carried out by Nazi Germany and Imperial Japan during WWII, these airstrikes do not distinguish between military and civilian targets, with entire neighborhoods reduced to rubble. The destruction of vital infrastructure is not merely collateral damage—it is a deliberate tactic to weaken Gaza's ability to sustain itself, pushing its people deeper into poverty and desperation.

The **denial of essential goods** under the blockade further exacerbates the situation. Gaza's economy is heavily dependent on imports, and the blockade has restricted everything from food and fuel to construction materials needed to rebuild after airstrikes. Fishing boats, which provide a critical source of food and livelihood for many Gazans, are restricted to a narrow zone by Israeli naval forces, cutting off access to larger fishing areas and severely limiting the amount of food that can be harvested. The blockade's control over agricultural inputs and exports has crippled Gaza's farming industry, leading to food insecurity and malnutrition among the population. This strategy of economic strangulation is reminiscent of Japan's occupation tactics during WWII, where food was systematically looted and diverted for military use, leaving the local population to starve.

The blockade also restricts access to **medical care**, with patients often unable to leave Gaza for life-saving treatments. Hospitals, already overwhelmed by shortages of medicine and equipment, struggle to cope with the constant influx of casualties from airstrikes and other forms of violence. The deliberate obstruction of medical supplies and the inability to evacuate patients in critical condition are stark reminders of the siege tactics used by Imperial Japan, where civilians were left to die from preventable diseases and starvation as a method of warfare.

Much like the **siege of Nanjing** or the **blockade of Warsaw**, the blockade of Gaza is a tool of collective punishment. While Israel claims its actions are in defense of its national security, the reality on the ground shows a systematic effort to degrade the living conditions of over two million civilians trapped within Gaza's borders. The blockade, combined with intermittent military strikes, has created a situation where civilians bear the brunt of the conflict, suffering from malnutrition, lack of medical care, and constant fear of bombardment. This form of modern siege warfare mirrors the brutal tactics of WWII, where civilian populations were deliberately targeted to weaken the enemy's resolve.

The **psychological impact** of the blockade cannot be ignored. Just as civilians under siege in WWII experienced the constant terror of air raids and starvation, the people of Gaza live in a state of perpetual uncertainty, knowing that any moment could bring another round of bombings or further restrictions on their already limited access to basic needs. The destruction of homes and infrastructure, combined with the inability to rebuild due to the lack of construction materials, leaves many Gazans with no hope for a better future. This cycle of destruction and deprivation is designed to break the spirit of the people, much like the WWII sieges that sought to demoralize populations into submission.

International human rights organizations have condemned the blockade of Gaza as a violation of international law, particularly the Fourth Geneva Convention, which prohibits collective punishment and requires the protection of civilians during times of war. Despite this, the blockade remains in place, with little relief for the people of Gaza. The parallels between Israel's tactics and those of Nazi Germany and Imperial Japan are clear: all three have used the deliberate targeting of civilians and the denial of essential goods as a means to control and subdue occupied populations.

In both past and present, the use of siege and starvation tactics leaves a lasting legacy of suffering, resentment, and trauma. The blockade of Gaza, much like the sieges of WWII, will be remembered as a dark chapter in modern history, where the suffering of innocent civilians was used as a weapon of war. The world must recognize these patterns and work to ensure that such tactics are condemned and prevented, not only for the sake of Gaza but for the future of all conflicts where civilians are trapped in the crossfire of political and military ambitions.

Chapter 4: Targeting Civilians: The Brutality of War Across Eras

In the midst of conflict, one of the most devastating tactics employed by military powers is the deliberate targeting of civilians. During World War II, both Nazi Germany and Imperial Japan unleashed brutal campaigns of bombings and massacres that inflicted unimaginable suffering on civilian populations. These attacks were designed to destroy morale, cripple infrastructure, and terrorize entire nations into submission. Civilians—men, women, and children—became pawns in a broader strategy of total war, where no distinction was made between combatants and non-combatants. In modern times, this same ruthless strategy can be seen in the Israeli-Palestinian conflict, where airstrikes in Gaza and the West Bank have systematically destroyed civilian infrastructure, leading to immense human suffering. Despite being separated by decades, these acts of violence share a common goal: breaking the will of a people by attacking the most vulnerable.

During World War II, Nazi Germany carried out **indiscriminate bombings and massacres** across Europe, targeting civilian populations with deliberate precision. In 1939, the siege of **Warsaw** saw the systematic bombing of the Polish capital by the German Luftwaffe. Civilians were caught in the crossfire as entire neighborhoods were flattened, hospitals destroyed, and countless lives lost. The bombing campaign was not just about military conquest—it was an assault on the city's people, aimed at crushing Polish resistance by breaking the civilian population. By targeting civilians, the Nazis sought to send a message of fear and helplessness, illustrating the consequences of defiance.

In 1940, the bombing of **Rotterdam** by German forces took this strategy to new heights. The city was bombed to the ground in less than two hours, with over 800 civilians killed and 85,000 left homeless. This devastating attack was launched not for military gain but as a form of psychological warfare, designed to force the Dutch government into submission. Rotterdam's destruction served as a warning to other European nations of what awaited them should they resist the Nazi war machine. The bombing of cities like Warsaw and Rotterdam was part of a broader pattern of Nazi brutality in occupied Europe, where civilian populations were systematically targeted to break their spirit.

Beyond the bombings, Nazi forces committed horrific **massacres** of civilians in occupied territories, such as the **mass shooting of civilians in Oradour-sur-Glane** in France and the systematic murder of entire villages in Eastern Europe in retaliation for acts of resistance. These atrocities were designed to terrorize civilians, making them live in constant fear that any act of defiance, however small, would result in mass slaughter. The deliberate targeting of civilians was not an unintended consequence of war—it was a core element of the Nazi strategy of domination through terror.

Imperial Japan's war crimes also involved the systematic bombing of civilian populations and the use of chemical weapons. During the Second Sino-Japanese War, Japanese forces carried out relentless bombing campaigns on Chinese cities, with **Chongqing** being one of the hardest hit. From 1938 to 1943, Chongqing endured hundreds of bombing raids that targeted civilian infrastructure, including schools, hospitals, and residential areas. The bombings caused tens of thousands of civilian deaths, and those who survived were left to pick up the pieces in a city ravaged by destruction. The goal, much like in Nazi Germany's campaigns, was to demoralize the population and force the Chinese government to capitulate. Civilian suffering was seen as an acceptable price to pay for military victory.

Japan also used **chemical weapons** against Chinese civilians, in clear violation of international law. These weapons were deployed in both rural and urban areas, leading to horrific injuries and death for non-combatants. The use of chemical weapons against civilians demonstrated the lengths to which Japan was willing to go in its pursuit of domination, using tools of war that inflicted maximum suffering on the most vulnerable members of society. Much like the bombings, the use of chemical weapons was part of a broader strategy to break the will of the Chinese people through relentless, inhumane tactics.

In modern times, the **Israeli airstrikes on Gaza and the West Bank** have drawn comparisons to these WWII-era tactics, as civilians continue to suffer disproportionately from military actions. In Gaza, airstrikes have frequently targeted densely populated areas, resulting in the destruction of homes, schools, hospitals, and other critical infrastructure. The **systematic destruction of civilian infrastructure** has left Gaza's population in a perpetual state of crisis, with limited access to clean water, electricity, and medical care. Just as Nazi bombings sought to cripple the infrastructure of European cities, Israeli airstrikes have devastated Gaza's ability to function as a society. Civilians are left to pick up the pieces in a region where rebuilding is nearly impossible due to ongoing blockades and restrictions on building materials.

The **toll on innocent lives** in Gaza is staggering. Airstrikes aimed at military targets often result in "collateral damage" where civilians, including children, are killed or injured. Homes are reduced to rubble, families displaced, and entire communities shattered. Much like the bombings of Warsaw and Chongqing, the civilians of Gaza are caught in the middle of a conflict where they are not only incidental victims but also deliberate targets. The destruction of vital infrastructure further exacerbates the humanitarian crisis, as hospitals struggle to treat the wounded and provide basic care amid power outages and shortages of essential medical supplies.

In the **West Bank**, Israeli airstrikes and military actions have similarly targeted civilian areas, particularly in the context of responding to acts of resistance or protest. The use of overwhelming force in these areas has drawn criticism from human rights organizations, which argue that the targeting of civilian populations violates international law and constitutes collective punishment. Just as the Nazis retaliated against civilian populations for resistance efforts, Israeli actions in the West Bank often result in disproportionate harm to civilians, creating a cycle of violence and retribution.

Across all these eras, the deliberate targeting of civilians serves as a tool of war, intended to break the will of a population by attacking its most vulnerable members. Whether it is through bombings, chemical weapons, or airstrikes, the aim is the same: to inflict enough suffering on civilians that the enemy is forced to capitulate. While the specifics of the conflicts may differ, the impact on civilians remains tragically consistent. The deliberate destruction of homes, schools, hospitals, and critical infrastructure leaves lasting scars on communities, perpetuating cycles of poverty, trauma, and instability long after the bombs have stopped falling.

Nazi Bombings and Massacres: The Deliberate Targeting of Civilians in Occupied Europe

DURING WORLD WAR II, Nazi Germany engaged in a strategy of total war that disregarded the distinction between military targets and civilian populations. Civilians became direct targets of violence through bombings, massacres, and punitive actions across occupied Europe. These deliberate attacks were not only aimed at undermining resistance efforts but were also intended to terrorize and subjugate entire nations. The bombing of cities like Warsaw and Rotterdam, along with brutal massacres in various occupied territories, exemplified the Nazis' willingness to use extreme measures against civilians as a tool of war.

One of the earliest and most devastating examples of Nazi bombings targeting civilians occurred in **Warsaw** in September 1939. As part of Germany's invasion of Poland, the Luftwaffe launched a relentless bombing campaign against the Polish capital. The attacks were designed not only to destroy military targets but to break the will of the Polish people by flattening entire residential areas. The bombing of Warsaw resulted in widespread destruction, with hospitals, schools, and homes reduced to rubble. Over 25,000 civilians were killed during the siege, and many more were left injured or homeless. The Nazis aimed to crush Polish resistance by creating an atmosphere of terror, signaling that any defiance would be met with overwhelming and indiscriminate force. The fall of Warsaw marked the beginning of a brutal occupation in which the targeting of civilians became a key tactic.

The bombing of **Rotterdam** in May 1940 was another egregious example of Nazi brutality against civilians. After a failed attempt to force the city's surrender through negotiations, the Luftwaffe was ordered to destroy the city. In less than two hours, much of Rotterdam was reduced to ashes. The bombardment was indiscriminate, with entire civilian districts obliterated by high-explosive bombs. Over 800 civilians were killed, and tens of thousands were left homeless. This act of terror was intended to break Dutch morale and force the surrender of the Netherlands. The destruction of Rotterdam was not just a military operation—it was a message to the world that Nazi Germany would stop at nothing to achieve its objectives, even if it meant annihilating civilian populations. Rotterdam's bombing set the stage for further air raids across Europe, where civilians would continue to suffer the consequences of Nazi expansionism.

Beyond these bombings, the Nazis also conducted widespread **massacres of civilians** in occupied territories, particularly as reprisals for resistance efforts. One of the most infamous atrocities occurred in the French village of **Oradour-sur-Glane** in June 1944. In retaliation for the activities of French resistance fighters, Nazi SS troops entered the village and systematically massacred 642 civilians, including women and children. Men were gathered in barns and shot, while women and children were locked inside the village church, which was then set on fire. Those who tried to escape were gunned down. The village was left in ruins, a chilling reminder of the Nazi policy of collective punishment. Similar massacres took place across occupied Europe, particularly in Poland and the Soviet Union, where entire villages were destroyed as a means of quelling resistance. The Nazis viewed civilians as legitimate targets if they believed those civilians were supporting or harboring partisans or resistance fighters.

The Nazi regime also used bombings and massacres to enforce control in **Eastern Europe**, where resistance movements were particularly strong. In the Soviet Union, the **Siege of Leningrad** stands as one of the most prolonged and deadly sieges in history. While not strictly a bombing campaign, the Nazi strategy involved cutting off the city's food and supply lines, leading to the starvation and death of over one million civilians. The deliberate targeting of civilians through sieges and bombardment was a core part of the Nazi strategy, aiming to weaken the resolve of entire populations by subjecting them to unimaginable suffering.

The pattern of **indiscriminate bombings and civilian massacres** that characterized Nazi military campaigns across Europe reflects the regime's commitment to total war, where the destruction of civilian life was seen as an acceptable means to achieve military and ideological goals. Civilians were not only collateral damage but were often the intended targets, used as leverage to force governments into submission or to punish resistance movements. The legacy of these bombings and massacres remains a haunting reminder of the extremes of wartime violence and the human cost of Nazi Germany's pursuit of domination.

The deliberate targeting of civilians during World War II by Nazi Germany laid bare the devastating impact of total war on innocent populations. By using civilians as pawns in their broader strategy of conquest, the Nazis left a trail of destruction that devastated families, communities, and entire nations. The bombings of Warsaw and Rotterdam, along with countless massacres, demonstrate how civilians were systematically targeted to demoralize and suppress any opposition to the Nazi regime, creating a legacy of terror that continues to echo through history.

Imperial Japan's Civilian Bombings: Chongqing and the Horrors of Chemical Warfare

DURING ITS AGGRESSIVE expansion across Asia in World War II, Imperial Japan employed brutal tactics that deliberately targeted civilian populations, causing widespread death and destruction. Among these tactics were relentless bombing campaigns on major cities, including Chongqing, which became a symbol of the suffering inflicted on non-combatants. In addition to aerial bombings, Japan violated international law by using chemical weapons against civilians, further demonstrating its willingness to use inhumane methods to achieve its military objectives. The targeting of civilians by Imperial Japan was not an incidental byproduct of war but a calculated strategy aimed at breaking the morale of both enemy forces and the civilian population.

The **bombing of Chongqing**, which began in 1938 and continued for five years, was one of the most devastating bombing campaigns against a civilian population during the Second Sino-Japanese War. As Japan sought to force China into submission, Chongqing, the wartime capital of the Chinese Nationalist government, became a primary target. Japanese bombers launched hundreds of raids on the city, dropping incendiary bombs designed to create widespread fires. Chongqing's dense population and wooden structures made it particularly vulnerable to such attacks. The bombings were indiscriminate, targeting residential areas, schools, hospitals, and markets, with little regard for civilian life.

The human toll of the **Chongqing bombings** was staggering. Tens of thousands of civilians were killed, with many burned alive in the fires caused by the bombings. Survivors were left to navigate a city in ruins, with bodies scattered in the streets and entire neighborhoods reduced to ashes. The Japanese strategy was clear: by targeting civilians, they hoped to cripple China's ability to continue the war by destroying the morale of the Chinese people. The bombings of Chongqing served no direct military purpose; they were designed to terrorize the population and create chaos in the heart of China's wartime government. Despite the onslaught, the Chinese government refused to surrender, and the city's people endured years of suffering under the relentless bombing raids.

In addition to the bombings, Imperial Japan's use of **chemical weapons** added another layer of horror to its war crimes against civilians. Chemical weapons, such as mustard gas and phosgene, were deployed in both combat zones and civilian areas, particularly in China. The use of chemical weapons against civilian populations was a direct violation of the Geneva Protocol, which prohibited the use of such weapons in warfare. However, Japan ignored these international laws, deploying chemical agents to cause mass casualties and widespread panic among civilians. These weapons caused horrific injuries, burning the skin, damaging the lungs, and leaving survivors with lifelong health complications.

The Japanese military's willingness to use **chemical weapons** was not limited to battlefield situations but extended to rural and urban civilian populations, further underscoring the regime's disregard for human life. Villages suspected of harboring resistance fighters or civilians caught in conflict zones were often targeted with chemical weapons, leaving entire communities devastated. In many cases, civilians had no means of protection against these attacks, and those exposed to the gas suffered agonizing deaths. The use of chemical weapons was another tool in Japan's broader strategy of terrorizing civilian populations to break their spirit and force surrender.

The bombing of Chongqing and the use of chemical weapons by Imperial Japan left a legacy of trauma and devastation across China. Civilians, who should have been protected under international law, became the primary victims of Japan's strategy of total war. The deliberate targeting of non-combatants through aerial bombings and chemical warfare mirrored the ruthless tactics used by Nazi Germany in Europe, further highlighting the global scale of atrocities committed during World War II. Imperial Japan's willingness to violate international norms and inflict mass suffering on civilians remains one of the darkest chapters of its wartime legacy.

The impact of these crimes is still felt today, as survivors of the bombings and chemical attacks continue to grapple with the physical and psychological scars left by Japan's wartime actions. The targeting of civilians through bombings and chemical weapons exemplifies the extreme lengths to which Imperial Japan was willing to go to achieve its imperialist ambitions, with little regard for the human cost. These tactics not only violated the rules of war but also stripped away any pretense of morality in Japan's military strategy, leaving a lasting mark on the history of warfare and civilian suffering.

Israel's Airstrikes on Gaza and the West Bank: The Destruction of Civilian Infrastructure and the Human Cost

IN THE LONG AND FRAUGHT history of the Israeli-Palestinian conflict, Israel's military actions, particularly its airstrikes on Gaza and the West Bank, have repeatedly targeted civilian infrastructure, causing immense suffering for innocent civilians. These airstrikes, often justified by the Israeli government as necessary responses to threats from militant groups like Hamas, have led to the widespread destruction of homes, schools, hospitals, and essential utilities. The toll on human life and the resulting humanitarian crises have drawn widespread international criticism, with many arguing that Israel's military campaigns disproportionately harm civilians, trapping entire populations in a cycle of violence and poverty.

The **airstrikes on Gaza**, in particular, have been devastating to the civilian population. Since 2007, Gaza has been subjected to repeated rounds of intense military bombardment by Israeli forces, with entire neighborhoods being reduced to rubble. One of the most significant impacts of these airstrikes has been the destruction of vital civilian infrastructure. Water treatment facilities, power plants, and sanitation systems have been destroyed or severely damaged, leaving millions of people without access to clean water, electricity, or basic health services. The resulting humanitarian crisis has left Gaza's population, already suffering under a blockade, in a state of perpetual hardship. The lack of essential infrastructure has also led to outbreaks of diseases, malnutrition, and a health system on the brink of collapse.

One of the most tragic consequences of these airstrikes is the destruction of **schools and hospitals**. In several instances, airstrikes have hit UN-run schools and hospitals, killing civilians, including children, who were sheltering from the violence. These attacks have not only destroyed places of learning and care but have also created an environment of fear where civilians have nowhere safe to turn. The trauma inflicted on children and families is profound, with entire generations growing up under the constant threat of bombings, severely affecting their mental health and well-being. In the densely populated Gaza Strip, where civilian infrastructure is often located near military targets, the risk of civilian casualties is high, leading to the loss of many innocent lives during these strikes.

The **West Bank** has also seen its share of airstrikes, particularly during escalations of violence or in response to perceived security threats. In the West Bank, airstrikes and military raids have targeted homes, government buildings, and infrastructure critical to daily life. The destruction of roads, bridges, and water supplies has made life for civilians even more difficult, compounding the effects of the Israeli occupation. In many cases, airstrikes and raids are followed by restrictions on movement, curfews, and military checkpoints, which further isolate communities and prevent the delivery of humanitarian aid.

Beyond the immediate physical destruction, the **psychological toll** on the civilian population is immense. Airstrikes create a constant state of fear and uncertainty, with civilians never knowing when or where the next attack will strike. The trauma of losing loved ones, witnessing the destruction of homes, or surviving an airstrike leaves deep scars on those affected. This psychological warfare, coupled with the physical devastation, has led to widespread anxiety, depression, and other mental health issues among Palestinians, particularly children. The repeated destruction of homes and the inability to rebuild due to restrictions on building materials exacerbate the despair felt by many families, leaving them trapped in a cycle of poverty and displacement.

Israel's airstrikes often target **infrastructure** that supports Gaza's economy, further crippling an already impoverished region. Factories, businesses, and agricultural facilities have been destroyed, making it difficult for Gaza's population to recover economically after each round of bombardments. The destruction of industrial and agricultural infrastructure has led to widespread unemployment, food insecurity, and a dependence on international aid. This economic strangulation, combined with the physical destruction of the territory, has left Gaza in a constant state of reconstruction, with little progress being made before the next wave of airstrikes hits.

International human rights organizations have repeatedly condemned the **disproportionate impact** of Israeli airstrikes on civilians and civilian infrastructure. While Israel maintains that it targets militant groups and their assets, the reality on the ground shows that civilians bear the brunt of these military actions. The high civilian death toll, the destruction of essential services, and the long-term damage to the region's infrastructure have raised serious questions about the legality and morality of these military operations. Critics argue that these airstrikes amount to collective punishment, as they disproportionately affect civilians who have no control over the actions of militant groups operating in the area.

The **human cost** of these airstrikes is profound. Thousands of civilians have lost their lives in the ongoing conflict, with many more injured or permanently disabled. Families are left to mourn loved ones, while others are displaced from their homes, forced to live in overcrowded shelters or refugee camps. The constant threat of airstrikes means that life in Gaza and parts of the West Bank is lived under the shadow of violence, with little hope for a peaceful and secure future.

The destruction caused by Israel's airstrikes on Gaza and the West Bank is not just a military strategy—it is a strategy that systematically undermines the ability of civilians to live with dignity. The loss of homes, the destruction of critical infrastructure, and the psychological trauma inflicted on millions of people have created a humanitarian disaster that shows no signs of abating. While Israel argues that these actions are necessary for its security, the overwhelming toll on innocent lives raises serious ethical and legal questions about the proportionality and justification of these attacks. The long-term impact on civilian populations will continue to shape the region for generations, deepening the cycle of violence and suffering in the Israeli-Palestinian conflict.

Chapter 5: Forced Displacement and Ethnic Cleansing: The Legacy of Population Control and Territorial Domination

Throughout history, forced displacement and ethnic cleansing have been used as powerful tools by regimes seeking to expand their control over territory and resources, often at the cost of displacing and erasing entire populations. These policies are rooted in the belief that by removing or relocating certain groups, a regime can reshape the demographic landscape to fit its ideological or territorial goals. Nazi Germany, Imperial Japan, and modern-day Israel have all employed such strategies, using forced relocations, deportations, and the destruction of homes and communities to establish control over contested areas. The consequences of these actions have been devastating, resulting in the loss of homes, livelihoods, and the cultural annihilation of targeted populations.

Nazi Germany's policies of **forced relocation and ethnic cleansing** were central to Adolf Hitler's vision of a greater Germany, one that would expand into Eastern Europe and establish a vast empire based on racial purity. This vision, known as **Lebensraum**, or "living space," involved the systematic removal of Slavic peoples, Jews, and other "undesirable" populations from their homelands to make way for ethnic Germans. The Nazis believed that Germans were the superior race and that they deserved to settle in Eastern Europe, which was to be "cleansed" of non-Germans. This policy led to the forced relocation of millions of people from their homes, either through deportation to concentration camps or by resettling them in labor camps.

In occupied territories such as **Poland** and **Czechoslovakia**, entire towns and villages were cleared of their inhabitants to make room for German settlers. Families were torn apart, forced onto trains, and relocated to ghettos or labor camps, where many would die from starvation, disease, or execution. The policy of Lebensraum was not just about territorial expansion—it was about **ethnic cleansing** on a massive scale. The ultimate goal was the complete eradication of non-Germans from these lands, and the consequences of this brutal policy were horrific, with millions of people losing their homes, their communities, and their lives.

Similarly, **Imperial Japan** also employed forced displacement and deportation as part of its efforts to expand its empire across Asia. As Japan occupied territories in **China**, **Korea**, **Southeast Asia**, and the **Pacific Islands**, it implemented a policy of forced deportations and relocations to exert control over the local populations and extract resources for its war effort. Civilians were moved across the empire, often to work in forced labor camps or serve the Japanese military. In **Korea**, thousands of men were forcibly conscripted into the Japanese army, while women were subjected to sexual slavery as "comfort women" for Japanese soldiers.

In occupied **China**, entire villages were cleared to make way for Japanese military bases or agricultural projects aimed at feeding Japan's war machine. Civilians who resisted deportation were often met with brutal force, including executions and mass killings. In other cases, the Japanese military conducted scorched-earth campaigns, destroying homes, farms, and infrastructure to prevent local populations from supporting resistance fighters. The forced displacement of civilians across Japan's empire was not only a tactic to consolidate control but also an attempt to erase local cultures and assimilate conquered peoples into the Japanese empire.

In **modern-day Israel**, the forced displacement of **Palestinians** has been a longstanding and controversial aspect of the Israeli-Palestinian conflict. Since the establishment of Israel in 1948, hundreds of thousands of Palestinians have been displaced from their homes through a combination of war, military occupation, and the expansion of Israeli settlements. The process of **settler expansion** in the **West Bank** has been particularly contentious, with Palestinian families evicted from their homes and their land appropriated to make way for Israeli settlers. Homes have been demolished, olive groves uprooted, and entire communities displaced, often with little or no compensation.

The construction of Israeli settlements in the **West Bank** and **East Jerusalem** is viewed by many as a form of **ethnic cleansing**, aimed at altering the demographic landscape of these contested areas. The Israeli government justifies these actions as necessary for security and the establishment of a Jewish homeland, but the impact on Palestinian civilians has been devastating. Families who have lived on their land for generations have been forcibly removed, their homes destroyed, and their communities fragmented. In some cases, entire villages have been demolished, leaving residents homeless and without recourse. The displacement of Palestinians is often accompanied by the seizure of their land for settlement construction, creating a situation in which Palestinians are systematically marginalized and denied basic rights.

The **displacement of Palestinians** has also been exacerbated by military actions, such as airstrikes and raids that target homes and civilian infrastructure. These actions, coupled with evictions and the construction of the **separation wall**, have created a situation in which Palestinians are effectively confined to small, isolated enclaves. The ongoing expansion of Israeli settlements, combined with the forced displacement of Palestinians, has been widely condemned by the international community as a violation of international law and human rights. Yet, the process continues, with Palestinians facing an uncertain future, unable to return to their homes or reclaim their land.

The use of **forced displacement and ethnic cleansing** by Nazi Germany, Imperial Japan, and Israel reveals a common thread: the belief that territorial control can be solidified by removing or erasing the populations that stand in the way. In all three cases, civilians have borne the brunt of these policies, losing their homes, their communities, and their sense of identity. The long-term effects of forced displacement are profound, leaving lasting scars on those who are displaced and creating a cycle of poverty, trauma, and instability that is difficult to overcome. Whether motivated by racial ideologies, imperial ambitions, or national security concerns, the forced relocation of civilians remains one of the most devastating consequences of conflict, with entire generations left to grapple with the loss of their homes and their future.

Nazi Germany's Forced Relocations: The Pursuit of Lebensraum and Ethnic Cleansing

NAZI GERMANY'S POLICY of forced relocations and ethnic cleansing was a central element of Adolf Hitler's vision for a new Europe, rooted in the concept of **Lebensraum**, or "living space." This ideological framework was based on the belief that the Aryan race, particularly Germans, deserved vast tracts of land in Eastern Europe to expand and prosper. To achieve this goal, Hitler and the Nazi regime initiated a campaign of forced displacement, designed to clear out entire populations of Slavs, Jews, Romani, and other "undesirables" to make way for German settlers. These relocations were not merely about land; they were about racial purity, and the systematic removal of people seen as inferior was a fundamental part of the Nazi war effort.

At the heart of the **Lebensraum** policy was the belief that Germany needed more land to grow and secure its future. Hitler viewed Eastern Europe, particularly areas like Poland, Ukraine, and Russia, as fertile territory for German colonization. To make room for German settlers, the native populations in these regions were to be forcibly removed, displaced, or exterminated. This policy of ethnic cleansing was carried out with ruthless efficiency, beginning with the invasion of Poland in 1939 and expanding as the German army advanced eastward.

In **Poland**, the Nazi occupation was marked by widespread displacement. Hundreds of thousands of Polish civilians were forcibly removed from their homes and deported to labor camps or ghettos. Entire towns and villages were cleared, with homes and farms taken over by German settlers. Those who were not deported often faced brutal treatment, as the Nazis sought to erase Polish culture and identity. Jewish Poles were particularly targeted, herded into ghettos under horrific conditions, while millions of others were sent to concentration camps where they were systematically murdered. The **Warsaw Ghetto**, one of the largest and most infamous, became a symbol of Nazi cruelty, where overcrowding, starvation, and disease led to the deaths of hundreds of thousands before the eventual mass deportations to death camps.

The Nazis also implemented their **Generalplan Ost**, a detailed blueprint for the colonization of Eastern Europe, which called for the removal of around 30 to 40 million people. This plan extended beyond Poland into the **Soviet Union**, where millions of Slavs, Jews, and other ethnic minorities were to be forcibly relocated or exterminated. The German army, often with the assistance of the **SS**, conducted mass executions, forced deportations, and the destruction of entire communities as they advanced into Soviet territory. Cities like **Kiev** and **Minsk** were targeted for ethnic cleansing, with their populations either deported or killed, and the land repurposed for German settlers.

In addition to the forced relocations, the Nazis engaged in widespread **ethnic cleansing** through brutal methods. The regime's racial policies dictated that non-Germans were inherently inferior, and thus had no right to exist on the land the Nazis sought to conquer. This led to the mass killing of millions of Jews, Slavs, Romani, and other groups through systematic genocide, including the use of concentration and death camps. While some populations were displaced, others were sent to forced labor camps to serve the German war machine, where they were worked to death in horrific conditions.

Operation Barbarossa, the invasion of the Soviet Union in 1941, significantly expanded the scope of Nazi relocations and ethnic cleansing efforts. As the German army swept across the Soviet countryside, they left a trail of destruction and displacement. The **Einsatzgruppen**, mobile killing squads, followed the army's advance, executing Jews, political dissidents, and other undesirables in mass shootings. Villages were burned, and the survivors were often deported to concentration camps or labor facilities. The plan for these territories was to replace the existing population with German settlers, creating a racially pure empire stretching across Europe.

The goal of Nazi forced relocations and **ethnic cleansing** was not just territorial conquest—it was the systematic reordering of Europe based on racist ideology. The Nazis believed that by eliminating or displacing entire populations, they could create a homogeneous, Aryan society that would dominate the continent. This vision led to the displacement of millions, the destruction of countless homes and communities, and the deaths of millions more through starvation, forced labor, and genocide.

The legacy of these forced relocations is one of immense human suffering. Entire cultures and communities were erased in the pursuit of Lebensraum, leaving a scar that has not healed. The forced deportations and ethnic cleansing carried out by the Nazis remain among the darkest chapters of World War II, illustrating the horrific consequences of ideologically driven policies that seek to reorder humanity according to race and nationality. For the survivors of these atrocities, the trauma of displacement, loss, and violence endures, reminding the world of the dangers of unchecked hatred and imperial ambition.

Imperial Japan's Forced Deportations: Civilian Displacement Across a Growing Empire

DURING ITS AGGRESSIVE expansion throughout Asia in World War II, **Imperial Japan** employed widespread forced deportations as a means of asserting control over conquered territories and mobilizing resources for its war effort. Civilians, particularly from occupied countries like **China**, **Korea**, and **Southeast Asia**, were forcibly relocated across Japan's empire to serve as laborers, soldiers, or, in many cases, victims of brutal exploitation. These deportations were driven by Japan's need to sustain its war machine, and they were often accompanied by violence, starvation, and the complete destruction of local communities. The forced movement of people was a key component of Japan's imperial ambitions, aimed at reshaping the demographic and economic landscape of its growing empire.

One of the most devastating examples of Japan's forced deportations occurred in **Korea**, which had been under Japanese colonial rule since 1910. As Japan ramped up its military campaigns in the 1930s and 1940s, it began conscripting hundreds of thousands of Korean civilians for forced labor and military service. These individuals were transported to Japan, **Manchuria**, and other parts of the empire, where they were subjected to inhumane working conditions in mines, factories, and construction sites. The work was grueling, and many deportees died from exhaustion, malnutrition, or abuse at the hands of their overseers. The conscription of Korean men into the Japanese military, often against their will, was another form of forced deportation, with many sent to the frontlines in dangerous and deadly combat situations.

Perhaps one of the most infamous aspects of Japan's forced deportation policies was the treatment of **"comfort women"**, a euphemistic term for the thousands of women, mostly from Korea, but also from China, the Philippines, and other occupied territories, who were forced into sexual slavery by the Japanese military. These women were deported to various military outposts across the empire, where they were subjected to repeated sexual violence and exploitation. Many of these women were taken under false pretenses, promised work or education, only to find themselves trapped in brutal conditions. The trauma inflicted on these women has left a lasting legacy, with survivors and their families continuing to seek justice for the crimes committed against them.

In **China**, Japan's forced deportations were part of a broader strategy of resource extraction and population control. As Japan sought to exploit the natural and human resources of China, large numbers of Chinese civilians were forcibly relocated to serve in labor camps or as agricultural workers. The deportations often followed Japan's scorched-earth military campaigns, in which entire villages were destroyed, and survivors were taken as forced labor. These deportees were sent to work in Japanese-controlled mines, railways, and factories, where they were subjected to brutal conditions, little food, and no medical care. Many died from malnutrition, disease, or overwork, while others were executed for failing to meet quotas or attempting to escape.

The forced deportation of civilians was not limited to **Korea** and **China**. Throughout **Southeast Asia**, particularly in territories such as the **Philippines, Indonesia**, and **Malaya**, Japan forcibly relocated civilians to work in labor camps and military facilities. In Indonesia, for instance, tens of thousands of civilians were forced to work on the construction of military infrastructure, including the infamous **Burma-Thailand Railway**, often referred to as the **"Death Railway."** This railway project became a symbol of Japan's cruel treatment of deported laborers, with more than 100,000 civilians and Allied prisoners of war dying from the horrific conditions they endured. The deported laborers were given little food, were forced to work long hours in extreme heat, and were frequently beaten or executed if they attempted to resist or escape.

In addition to labor deportations, Japan's forced relocation policies also sought to **restructure the population** in its occupied territories. In **Manchuria**, Japan attempted to create a Japanese-dominated colony by forcibly moving tens of thousands of Japanese civilians into the region, displacing the local Chinese and Manchu populations. This demographic reshaping was designed to assert Japanese cultural and political control over the region, reinforcing Japan's imperial dominance. The local populations were often moved to less fertile or resource-poor areas, stripping them of their livelihoods and forcing them into conditions of poverty and hardship.

Japan's **forced deportations** were a key part of its larger imperial strategy, designed to extract maximum resources from occupied territories while exerting control over local populations. The movement of civilians across the empire was often accompanied by brutal repression, as those who resisted deportation were frequently executed or imprisoned. The **inhumane conditions** faced by deported civilians, whether in labor camps, military service, or as victims of sexual slavery, resulted in untold suffering and death. These deportations were not only a violation of international law but also a grave humanitarian crisis that left a lasting impact on the millions of individuals who were forcibly displaced by Japan's imperial ambitions.

The legacy of **Japan's forced deportations** continues to be felt today, as many survivors and their descendants continue to seek justice and recognition for the crimes committed against them. The physical and psychological trauma inflicted on these populations, combined with the economic devastation caused by their forced displacement, has left deep scars on the countries and communities affected. Imperial

Japan's forced deportations stand as a stark reminder of the human cost of imperialism and war, where entire populations can be uprooted, exploited, and left to suffer in the name of territorial expansion and resource extraction.

Israel's Settler Expansion and the Displacement of Palestinians: Evictions, Home Demolitions, and Land Appropriation

THE DISPLACEMENT OF Palestinians due to Israel's settler expansion has been a central and deeply contentious issue in the Israeli-Palestinian conflict. For decades, Israeli settlements in the **West Bank** and **East Jerusalem** have expanded, resulting in the forced eviction of Palestinian families, the demolition of homes, and the appropriation of land. These actions have not only altered the demographic and geographic landscape of the region but have also exacerbated tensions, fueling a sense of injustice and despair among Palestinians. The process of settling Israeli citizens in occupied Palestinian territories is viewed by many as a form of **ethnic displacement**, aiming to establish permanent Israeli control over land that Palestinians have lived on for generations.

One of the most visible and impactful aspects of Israel's **settler expansion** is the **eviction of Palestinian families** from their homes. These evictions often occur under the guise of legal disputes, where Israeli courts, citing historical claims or property rights, rule in favor of Israeli settlers, ordering the removal of Palestinian residents. This has been especially prevalent in **East Jerusalem**, where Palestinian families have been forcibly evicted from neighborhoods like **Sheikh Jarrah** and **Silwan**. In many cases, these evictions result in families being displaced from homes they have lived in for decades, with little or no compensation. The eviction process is frequently accompanied by violence, as Israeli security forces enforce court rulings, leading to clashes with residents and protests from the local and international community.

The **demolition of Palestinian homes** has been another critical component of Israel's displacement policies. Thousands of Palestinian homes in the **West Bank** and **East Jerusalem** have been demolished under the pretext of lacking proper building permits, which are notoriously difficult for Palestinians to obtain due to Israeli-imposed restrictions. These demolitions often occur without warning, leaving families homeless and without resources to rebuild. The demolition of homes is not limited to urban areas but also affects **Bedouin** communities and rural villages, where entire communities have been displaced to make way for settlement expansion or military zones. For many Palestinians, the destruction of their homes is not just a loss of property, but a traumatic event that severs their connection to their land and community, contributing to a broader sense of disenfranchisement.

The **appropriation of Palestinian land** for Israeli settlements has been a driving force behind the displacement of Palestinians. Since the 1967 occupation of the **West Bank**, Israel has established hundreds of settlements, which now house hundreds of thousands of Israeli settlers. These settlements are often built on land confiscated from Palestinians, either through military orders or by declaring the land as "state land" under Israeli law. The construction of settlements not only displaces Palestinians from their homes but also fragments Palestinian communities, cutting off access to farmland, water resources, and essential services. The expansion of settlements is often accompanied by the construction of roads and infrastructure that further isolates Palestinian villages, creating a patchwork of disconnected territories that undermines the possibility of a contiguous Palestinian state.

One of the most significant impacts of settlement expansion has been the creation of **settler-only roads** and the construction of the **separation wall**, which divides many Palestinian communities from their land and restricts their movement. The wall, along with checkpoints and other security measures, has made it increasingly difficult for Palestinians to access agricultural land, travel to work or school, and maintain social and family connections. This fragmentation of the Palestinian territories has led to a growing sense of confinement and despair, as Palestinians find themselves living under what many describe as a system of **apartheid**, where their freedom of movement and access to resources are severely restricted.

The displacement caused by Israel's settlement policies has had profound **humanitarian consequences**. Families who are evicted or have their homes demolished are often left without shelter or support, forced to live in temporary housing or with relatives. The destruction of homes and the appropriation of land also have deep psychological effects, as Palestinians struggle with the loss of their heritage, identity, and connection to their ancestral land. The constant threat of eviction or demolition creates a climate of fear and instability, where Palestinians are unsure if they will be able to remain in their homes or if they will be the next to face displacement.

International law has repeatedly condemned Israel's settlement policies and the forced displacement of Palestinians. The **Fourth Geneva Convention** explicitly prohibits an occupying power from transferring its civilian population into the territory it occupies, and the United Nations has declared Israeli settlements in the West Bank and East Jerusalem illegal under international law. Despite these condemnations, settlement expansion continues, and with it, the displacement of Palestinians. The lack of accountability and enforcement of international law has allowed the situation to persist, deepening the divide between Israelis and Palestinians and making the prospect of a peaceful resolution to the conflict increasingly difficult.

The **displacement of Palestinians** as a result of Israel's settler expansion is not just a matter of property rights or legal disputes; it is a part of a broader strategy to reshape the demographic and geographic landscape of the region. By expanding settlements and displacing Palestinians, Israel solidifies its control over key areas of the West Bank and East Jerusalem, making the possibility of a two-state solution ever more remote. For Palestinians, the loss of their homes, land, and communities represents not only a physical displacement but also a loss of their future, as they are increasingly marginalized in a land they have called home for centuries.

The ongoing displacement of Palestinians through evictions, home demolitions, and land appropriation continues to be one of the most pressing issues in the Israeli-Palestinian conflict. As settlements expand and more land is taken, the possibility of peace and coexistence becomes more distant. The international community must address the root causes of this displacement and work toward a solution that respects the rights and dignity of both Israelis and Palestinians, ensuring that future generations do not continue to suffer the consequences of forced displacement and the appropriation of land.

Chapter 6: Segregation and Apartheid: Policies of Control and Exclusion Across Eras

Throughout history, segregation and apartheid have been used as powerful tools by regimes seeking to enforce racial, ethnic, or political dominance over certain groups. These systems of separation are rooted in ideologies of superiority, where one group is elevated above others and given exclusive rights and privileges. Whether through the ghettos and concentration camps of Nazi Germany, the ethnic policies of Imperial Japan, or the separation walls and checkpoints in modern Israel, segregation has consistently been employed to control, isolate, and oppress. These measures create systems of inequality, where the targeted populations are stripped of their basic human rights, restricted in their movements, and cut off from opportunities for prosperity or even survival.

In **Nazi Germany**, the segregation of **Jews** was a core part of Adolf Hitler's racial ideology. From the beginning of the Nazi regime, Jews were systematically excluded from public life and forced into segregated communities. The establishment of **ghettos** across Nazi-occupied Europe was one of the most visible manifestations of this segregation. In cities like **Warsaw** and **Lodz**, Jews were forcibly relocated to walled-off areas where they were subjected to inhumane conditions. The ghettos were overcrowded, with inadequate food, water, and medical supplies. The purpose was not only to isolate Jews but to slowly exterminate them through starvation, disease, and exposure. The ghettos served as holding areas for Jews before they were transported to **concentration camps** and **extermination camps**, where the final phase of the Holocaust was carried out.

The segregation of Jews was not just about physical separation; it was also about dehumanization. Jews in Nazi Germany were stripped of their citizenship, forced to wear the **yellow Star of David**, and denied basic legal protections. They were excluded from public life, schools, and jobs, relegated to the margins of society. The ghettos and concentration camps were an extreme form of segregation, designed to eradicate an entire ethnic group. The Nazi segregation policies did not just control movement; they aimed to destroy the Jewish population in its entirety. The horrors of the Holocaust stand as one of the darkest chapters of racial segregation in history, where systematic isolation was a precursor to genocide.

In **Imperial Japan**, ethnic segregation was also a key part of its imperial ambitions. As Japan sought to expand its empire across **East Asia**, it implemented policies of **racial superiority** and ethnic control, particularly in occupied territories such as **Korea, China**, and **Manchuria**. Japanese leaders believed in the inherent superiority of the Japanese race and sought to impose this ideology on the peoples they conquered. In **Manchuria**, Japan established a puppet state, **Manchukuo**, where ethnic Chinese and Manchu populations were subjugated to Japanese settlers. Japanese citizens were given privileged status, while local populations were forced into lower-tier jobs, denied access to education, and restricted in their movements. This segregation extended to physical spaces, where Japanese settlers lived in better housing and had access to superior infrastructure, while the local populations were confined to impoverished areas.

In **Korea**, Japan's colonial rule was marked by efforts to erase Korean identity and culture through **assimilation policies** that segregated Koreans from their Japanese rulers. Koreans were forced to adopt Japanese names, speak Japanese in schools, and abandon their own cultural practices. Ethnic segregation was enforced through a hierarchical system that placed Japanese citizens at the top and Koreans at the bottom. The segregation policies of Imperial Japan were not as overtly violent as the Nazi ghettos, but they were deeply oppressive, creating a system in which non-Japanese people were viewed as inferior and systematically excluded from the benefits of Japanese rule.

In the modern era, comparisons are often drawn between historical segregation and the current situation in **Israel and the Palestinian territories**, where the construction of **separation walls** and the proliferation of **checkpoints** have created a system that many describe as **apartheid**. The **Israeli separation barrier**, often referred to as the **apartheid wall** by critics, snakes through the **West Bank**, cutting off Palestinian communities from each other and from their land. The wall was originally constructed as a security measure, ostensibly to prevent terrorist attacks, but its path frequently deviates deep into Palestinian territory, encircling towns and villages and separating farmers from their fields. The wall has created a situation where Palestinians are unable to travel freely, with many having to apply for permits to access land, work, or visit family members on the other side of the barrier.

Alongside the wall, the extensive network of **military checkpoints** further restricts Palestinian movement. These checkpoints, often staffed by Israeli soldiers, control access between Palestinian areas and Israel or between different parts of the West Bank. For Palestinians, daily life is shaped by the checkpoints—waiting in long lines, enduring humiliating security checks, and sometimes being denied passage for arbitrary reasons. This system of control, while justified by the Israeli government as necessary for security, has been widely criticized as a form of **collective punishment**, trapping Palestinians in isolated enclaves where they are unable to access basic services or engage in economic activities. The restrictions on movement are seen as a means of exerting control over the Palestinian population, limiting their ability to resist Israeli occupation and settlement expansion.

The separation wall and checkpoints in Israel mirror historical systems of segregation in several ways. Like the ghettos of Nazi Germany or the segregated areas of Imperial Japan's colonies, the wall creates a physical barrier between two populations, reinforcing a system of inequality. The **expropriation of Palestinian land** for the construction of the wall and the **expansion of Israeli settlements** further erodes the possibility of a Palestinian state, much as the displacement of Jews in Nazi ghettos or the forced assimilation of Koreans under Japanese rule sought to erase the identity and autonomy of the oppressed populations.

The policies of **segregation and apartheid** in Israel and the Palestinian territories have drawn widespread international condemnation. Critics argue that the restrictions on Palestinian movement and the separation of communities create a system of racial and ethnic exclusion that mirrors some of the worst segregationist practices of the 20th century. The enduring impact of the wall and checkpoints is a sense of isolation, frustration, and despair among Palestinians, who are effectively cut off from the rest of the world and confined to fragmented territories under military control.

Segregation, whether in Nazi Germany, Imperial Japan, or modern Israel, serves the same purpose: to control and dominate a population by limiting their rights, restricting their movement, and isolating them from society. The walls, camps, and checkpoints that define these systems of exclusion are more than just physical barriers—they are symbols of the profound inequalities and injustices that arise when one group seeks to subjugate another. The consequences of segregation are far-reaching, creating lasting divisions and perpetuating cycles of violence and oppression that can take generations to overcome.

Nazi Segregation of Jews: The Brutal Reality of Ghettos and Concentration Camps

THE **Nazi regime's segregation of Jews** during World War II was one of the most systematic and brutal forms of racial discrimination in history. Under Adolf Hitler's leadership, the Nazi government sought to isolate, persecute, and ultimately annihilate Europe's Jewish population through a combination of forced segregation, deprivation, and mass murder. Central to this strategy were the establishment of **ghettos** and **concentration camps**, which served as key instruments in the Nazi plan to separate Jews from the rest of society, degrade their humanity, and, eventually, exterminate them.

The process of segregating Jews began shortly after the Nazis came to power in 1933, with a series of discriminatory laws and decrees designed to exclude Jews from public life. Over time, this exclusion evolved into the physical separation of Jews from non-Jews, which took its most extreme form in the creation of **ghettos**. These ghettos were urban districts in cities across Nazi-occupied Europe where Jews were forcibly relocated and confined under appalling conditions. The most infamous of these ghettos included the **Warsaw Ghetto** in Poland and the **Lodz Ghetto**.

The **Warsaw Ghetto**, established in 1940, was the largest of its kind. More than 400,000 Jews were crammed into a walled-off section of the city, cut off from the outside world. Life inside the ghetto was marked by severe overcrowding, with multiple families often forced to live in a single room. Sanitation was virtually non-existent, and disease, particularly typhus, spread rapidly. Food was scarce, with rations intentionally kept at starvation levels by the Nazi authorities. Jews in the ghetto were not allowed to leave, and the penalty for attempting to escape was death. Thousands died from hunger and disease long before they could be deported to death camps. The ghettos were not just prisons; they were designed to degrade and dehumanize Jews, reducing them to conditions where survival itself became a daily struggle.

The **ghettos** also served as a staging ground for the next phase of the Nazis' plan: the **Final Solution**, the mass deportation and extermination of Jews. Beginning in 1942, Jews from the ghettos were systematically rounded up and transported to **concentration camps** and **extermination camps**. The most notorious of these camps was **Auschwitz-Birkenau**, located in German-occupied Poland. Here, Jews were either immediately killed in gas chambers or subjected to forced labor, starvation, and brutal medical experiments.

The **concentration camps** were not merely prisons; they were the epicenter of the Nazi genocide. Upon arrival, Jews were subjected to selections, where those deemed unfit for labor—primarily the elderly, sick, women, and children—were sent directly to the gas chambers. Those who were spared immediate execution faced horrific conditions in the camps. Prisoners were forced to perform backbreaking labor on starvation rations, and many succumbed to disease, exhaustion, and mistreatment. The concentration camps were places of unimaginable suffering, where human life was devalued to the point of industrialized killing.

The **segregation** of Jews through ghettos and concentration camps was not only a means of controlling and isolating the Jewish population but also part of the Nazis' broader ideological mission of racial purification. Jews were dehumanized, labeled as subhuman, and treated as a threat to the purity of the Aryan race. This racial segregation was not just physical but psychological, as the Nazis sought to strip Jews of their dignity, identity, and basic human rights. The ghettos and concentration camps became symbols of the ultimate cruelty of the Nazi regime, where millions of innocent people were confined, brutalized, and killed simply because of their ethnicity.

The Nazi segregation of Jews represents one of the darkest chapters in human history. The systematic use of ghettos and concentration camps revealed the horrifying extent to which a state could institutionalize racism and hatred, leading to the deaths of six million

Jews in what came to be known as the **Holocaust**. The ghettos and concentration camps were not just places of segregation; they were instruments of genocide, designed to erase an entire people from existence.

Imperial Japan's Ethnic Segregation: Racial Superiority and the Control of Conquered Peoples

DURING THE EARLY 20TH century, Imperial Japan pursued an aggressive campaign of expansion across East Asia and the Pacific, driven by a belief in its own racial and cultural superiority. This expansionist ideology, known as **Pan-Asianism**, presented Japan as the leader of a new Asian order, where the Japanese race would dominate and "liberate" other Asian nations from Western colonialism. In reality, Japan's policies of racial superiority and ethnic segregation mirrored the oppressive practices of colonialism, as the Japanese military and government sought to control and exploit the populations of the territories they conquered. These policies not only created a rigid racial hierarchy but also subjected millions of people to discrimination, forced labor, and cultural erasure.

The foundation of Japan's ethnic segregation policies lay in its belief in the superiority of the **Yamato race**, which the Japanese considered to be the purest and most advanced race in Asia. This racial ideology justified Japan's imperial ambitions, positioning it as the rightful leader of an empire that would stretch from **Manchuria** to **Southeast Asia**. Under this system, Japanese settlers and officials were seen as the civilizing force, while the indigenous populations of Korea, China, and other occupied territories were viewed as racially and culturally inferior. This belief in racial superiority led to the implementation of segregationist policies that divided society along racial lines, granting privileges and rights to Japanese citizens while oppressing the local populations.

In **Korea**, which had been under Japanese colonial rule since 1910, the Japanese government implemented policies aimed at assimilating Koreans into Japanese culture while simultaneously maintaining a clear racial hierarchy. Koreans were forced to adopt Japanese names, speak the Japanese language, and abandon their own cultural traditions. Schools were segregated, with Japanese children receiving superior education and resources, while Korean children were taught a limited curriculum designed to promote obedience and loyalty to the empire. The Korean people were subjected to forced labor, particularly during World War II, when hundreds of thousands of Koreans were conscripted to work in Japanese factories or serve in the military under harsh conditions.

The situation in **Manchuria**, where Japan established the puppet state of **Manchukuo** in 1932, further exemplified Japan's policies of ethnic segregation and control. In Manchuria, Japanese settlers were given privileged status, occupying the best lands and enjoying superior infrastructure, while the local **Chinese** and **Manchu** populations were relegated to subordinate roles. Japanese settlers lived in separate, well-maintained communities, while the indigenous populations were subjected to strict curfews, restricted movement, and limited access to education and employment. The Japanese government's goal was to create a **colonial society** where Japanese settlers would dominate both economically and politically, while the local population would serve as a labor force to support the empire.

Japan's **racial policies** extended to its wartime occupations across **China**, **Southeast Asia**, and the **Pacific Islands**. In **China**, where Japan waged a brutal war of conquest, the Japanese military implemented policies that reinforced ethnic divisions between the Japanese occupiers and the Chinese population. Chinese civilians were often treated as second-class citizens, subjected to forced labor, summary executions, and widespread sexual violence. The infamous **Nanjing Massacre**, where Japanese soldiers raped, tortured, and killed tens of thousands of Chinese civilians, was a direct result of the belief in racial superiority that dehumanized the Chinese people in the eyes of the Japanese military.

In territories such as the **Philippines**, **Indonesia**, and **Malaya**, Japan's policies of racial segregation were also evident. Indigenous populations were often forced to work in mines, plantations, and infrastructure projects to support Japan's war effort, while Japanese settlers and military personnel occupied the upper echelons of society. Local elites who collaborated with the Japanese occupiers were sometimes given limited privileges, but the vast majority of the population faced severe repression, forced labor, and cultural erasure. In these territories, Japan's racial policies were justified through the rhetoric of "Asian unity," but in practice, they resulted in the exploitation and oppression of millions of people.

A particularly insidious aspect of Japan's ethnic segregation policies was the forced recruitment of **comfort women**, a euphemism for the tens of thousands of women, primarily from Korea, China, and the Philippines, who were forced into sexual slavery by the Japanese military. These women, who were often kidnapped or coerced, were segregated from Japanese society and forced to serve Japanese soldiers in military brothels across the empire. The comfort women system was a manifestation of the broader racial hierarchy imposed by Japan, where non-Japanese women were viewed as disposable and inferior.

Imperial Japan's policies of **ethnic segregation** were not only a tool of control but also a means of reinforcing Japanese identity and superiority over the peoples it conquered. By segregating and dehumanizing the local populations, Japan was able to justify its harsh colonial rule and exploit the resources and labor of its empire. These policies left a lasting legacy of trauma and division in the regions affected, and they serve as a stark reminder of the dangers of racial superiority and segregationist ideologies.

In the aftermath of Japan's defeat in World War II, many of these policies were dismantled, but the scars of Japan's racial hierarchy and segregationist practices continue to affect the countries that were once part of its empire. The legacy of ethnic control, forced assimilation, and exploitation remains a contentious issue in relations between Japan and its former colonies, particularly in **Korea** and **China**, where the memories of Japan's racial policies are still vividly remembered.

Israeli Separation Walls and Checkpoints: Modern Segregation and the Restriction of Palestinian Movement

THE CONSTRUCTION OF **separation walls** and the establishment of an extensive network of **checkpoints** in the Israeli-occupied **West Bank** and around **East Jerusalem** have created a system of control that has drawn comparisons to historical forms of segregation, particularly those employed during World War II. While differing in context and scale, the core principle of limiting the movement of an oppressed group through physical barriers and checkpoints bears similarities to the methods used by Nazi Germany to segregate and control populations during the Holocaust. In the modern era, Israel's separation walls and checkpoints serve to isolate Palestinian communities, restrict their access to essential services, and enforce a system of segregation that many critics describe as a form of **apartheid**.

One of the most significant manifestations of this system is the **Israeli separation barrier**, a vast structure that stretches over 700 kilometers, cutting through the West Bank and encircling parts of East Jerusalem. Officially, the barrier is presented by the Israeli government as a **security measure**, designed to prevent attacks by Palestinian militants. However, the path of the wall often extends deep into

Palestinian territory, far beyond the 1967 borders, encircling Palestinian villages and separating them from their agricultural land, schools, and healthcare services. The result is the effective **segregation** of Palestinians, creating isolated enclaves that are cut off from the rest of the West Bank and, in many cases, from each other.

The impact of the **separation wall** on Palestinian daily life is profound. Farmers are often separated from their land, requiring permits to access fields that have been their source of livelihood for generations. Schools and hospitals located on the other side of the wall become inaccessible without passing through heavily guarded military checkpoints, which are frequently subject to arbitrary closures. This form of segregation is not merely about limiting movement; it is about restricting access to resources and services essential to a functioning society. The wall physically and symbolically divides Palestinians from their land, their heritage, and their communities.

The **checkpoints** that dot the West Bank and control access to East Jerusalem further exacerbate the segregation of Palestinians. These checkpoints, which number in the hundreds, are staffed by Israeli soldiers who regulate the movement of Palestinians, often with little transparency or consistency. Palestinians traveling between cities or villages within the West Bank, or attempting to enter Israel for work, medical care, or family visits, are forced to pass through these checkpoints. Long waits, intrusive searches, and the constant threat of being turned away are common experiences for Palestinians at these crossings.

The **restrictions on movement** imposed by the checkpoints are particularly harsh for those living in rural areas, who often rely on access to larger cities for healthcare, education, and employment. Many Palestinians are unable to reach hospitals in time during medical emergencies due to delays at checkpoints. Similarly, students and workers face daily uncertainty about whether they will be allowed to pass through checkpoints to reach their schools or jobs. This system creates a **fragmented existence** for Palestinians, where the simple act of traveling from one place to another becomes a challenge fraught with obstacles, leading to a profound sense of alienation and powerlessness.

The system of walls and checkpoints serves as a form of **modern segregation**, where Palestinians are confined to restricted areas while Israeli settlers and citizens enjoy freedom of movement. Israeli settlements, which continue to expand in the West Bank, are often connected by **settler-only roads**, bypassing Palestinian villages and checkpoints entirely. This creates a two-tiered system where Israelis have access to modern infrastructure and mobility, while Palestinians are subjected to control and restriction. The parallel with historical forms of segregation, particularly during **Nazi Germany**, lies in the deliberate isolation of a population based on ethnic or national identity, limiting their rights, movement, and access to basic services.

The **comparison to WWII-era segregation**, particularly the use of ghettos and walled-off areas to isolate Jews during the Holocaust, arises from the visible and psychological impact of these barriers. In Nazi-occupied Europe, Jews were forced into ghettos, where their movement was strictly controlled, and they were cut off from the rest of society. The walled ghettos served not only to isolate but also to dehumanize Jews, stripping them of their rights and reducing them to a marginalized existence. While the circumstances of the Israeli-Palestinian conflict differ, the **separation wall** in the West Bank has a similar effect of isolating Palestinians, restricting their freedoms, and reducing their access to the basic necessities of life.

Critics of the Israeli separation policies argue that the **checkpoints** and **walls** amount to a form of **apartheid**, a term used to describe the racial segregation policies of South Africa, where the white minority government enforced strict separation between racial groups. In the case of Israel, the physical barriers and restrictions on movement create a system where Palestinians are effectively segregated from Israelis, with different legal systems, rights, and freedoms depending on one's ethnicity and nationality. International human rights organizations have condemned the **separation wall** and the checkpoint system, calling for an end to the policies that isolate and oppress Palestinians.

The **human cost** of this segregation is immense. Families are separated, livelihoods are destroyed, and entire communities are left in limbo, unable to plan for their future. The constant presence of walls, fences, and military checkpoints creates a pervasive atmosphere of tension and fear, where Palestinians live under the constant gaze of the Israeli military. The walls and checkpoints are not just physical barriers; they are symbols of a system designed to control, oppress, and divide.

While Israel defends the separation barrier as a necessary security measure, the reality on the ground for Palestinians is one of **daily humiliation, restriction, and segregation**. The parallels with WWII-era segregation, particularly the use of walls and checkpoints to control and isolate populations, highlight the enduring power of physical barriers as tools of oppression. Whether in the form of ghettos in Nazi-occupied Europe or the separation wall in the West Bank, these barriers serve to strip people of their dignity, freedom, and humanity.

Chapter 7: Destruction of Cultural Identity: Erasing History to Assert Control

Throughout history, conquering powers have often sought not only to dominate populations militarily but also to erase the cultural identities of those they subjugate. By destroying cultural landmarks, suppressing languages, and rewriting histories, these regimes aim to weaken the spirit of the people they control, stripping them of their heritage and sense of belonging. The Nazis, Imperial Japan, and modern Israel have all engaged in policies designed to erase or suppress the cultural identities of the populations they sought to control. This systematic destruction of cultural identity is a powerful form of oppression, as it not only robs people of their past but also shapes their future by erasing the markers of their historical and cultural existence.

The **Nazi regime** pursued the deliberate **erasure of Jewish culture** as part of its broader genocidal campaign against the Jews of Europe. From the moment Hitler rose to power, Jewish culture and history were targeted for destruction alongside the physical annihilation of the Jewish people. The Nazis viewed Jewish culture as an existential threat to their vision of a racially pure Aryan state, and thus they sought to eliminate every trace of Jewish history, religion, and tradition from European society.

Jewish **synagogues**, **cemeteries**, and **cultural institutions** were systematically destroyed across Nazi-occupied Europe. In **Kristallnacht** (the Night of Broken Glass) in 1938, hundreds of synagogues were burned to the ground, Jewish businesses were ransacked, and cultural artifacts were stolen or destroyed. Jewish cemeteries were desecrated, gravestones were smashed, and religious objects, such as Torah scrolls, were confiscated or burned. The Nazis also looted Jewish libraries, museums, and art collections, stealing valuable cultural artifacts and works of art while discarding anything they deemed irrelevant to their Aryan agenda.

The Nazis' destruction of Jewish culture went hand in hand with their efforts to strip Jews of their identity. Jews were forced to wear the **yellow Star of David** as a means of marking them as different, and Jewish names were changed or removed from official records. Jewish intellectuals, artists, and scholars were silenced, their works banned, and their contributions erased from public life. The ghettos and concentration camps, where Jews were confined and killed, became the final places where Jewish culture could be expressed, but even in these horrific conditions, Jews attempted to preserve their traditions through clandestine schools, religious ceremonies, and cultural activities. Despite these efforts, the Nazi campaign to destroy Jewish culture was devastating, leaving a cultural void that the Jewish people have spent decades working to rebuild.

Imperial Japan also engaged in the **suppression of cultural identity** in the territories it conquered, particularly in **Korea**, **Taiwan**, and parts of **China**. Japan's imperial ambitions were built on the idea of **Pan-Asianism**, which, in theory, promoted Asian unity under Japanese leadership. However, in practice, this unity meant the forced **assimilation** of conquered peoples into Japanese culture, often through violent means. The Japanese viewed their own culture as superior and sought to replace local traditions and languages with their own.

In **Korea**, Japan imposed a policy of **cultural erasure** that sought to eliminate Korean identity entirely. Koreans were forced to adopt Japanese names, speak the Japanese language, and abandon their cultural traditions. Korean **schools** were required to teach Japanese history and culture, while Korean history, language, and customs were either ignored or actively suppressed. Koreans were also pressured to practice **Shintoism**, the state religion of Japan, in place of their own spiritual and religious practices. The goal was to create a population that was loyal to Japan and no longer identified with Korean culture or history.

In **Taiwan** and parts of **China**, Japan implemented similar policies of forced cultural assimilation. In Taiwan, Japanese authorities sought to replace the local language with Japanese, establishing schools where only Japanese was taught and where Taiwanese students were indoctrinated into Japanese cultural values. Taiwanese and Chinese cultural practices, including religious ceremonies, were discouraged or outright banned, as Japan attempted to impose its own identity on the people of these regions.

In occupied **China**, Japan's **cultural suppression** took on even more violent forms, particularly during the infamous **Nanjing Massacre**. In addition to the physical atrocities committed against the Chinese people, Japanese forces systematically looted and destroyed cultural landmarks, including temples, libraries, and historical sites. The goal was not just to conquer China militarily but to erase Chinese identity and replace it with Japanese cultural dominance.

In modern times, **Israel's targeting of Palestinian culture** has become a highly contentious issue, particularly in the context of the ongoing Israeli-Palestinian conflict. Israel's policies toward Palestinian cultural sites and heritage have been criticized as part of a broader strategy to assert control over the land and diminish the presence of Palestinian history in the region.

One aspect of this cultural targeting is the **destruction of Palestinian historical sites**. In areas such as **East Jerusalem** and the **West Bank**, Palestinian homes, mosques, and other cultural landmarks have been demolished, often under the justification of security concerns or lack of building permits. These demolitions not only displace Palestinians from their land but also erase their historical connection to these places. The destruction of **Muslim and Christian religious sites** in particular has drawn widespread international condemnation, as these sites are important not only to Palestinians but to the global religious community.

In addition to physical destruction, there is the issue of **renaming cities and towns** with Hebrew names, a process that some Palestinians and critics see as an attempt to overwrite Palestinian history. Palestinian towns with centuries-old Arabic names have been renamed in Hebrew, which erases the historical and cultural ties that Palestinians have to these places. This renaming is seen by many as an effort to present the land as historically Jewish, despite its long-standing multicultural history.

Historical revisionism is another significant element in the cultural conflict between Israel and the Palestinians. Some Israeli narratives emphasize the historical Jewish connection to the land while downplaying or erasing the contributions and presence of Palestinians throughout history. This form of historical revisionism shapes public perceptions and policies, leading to the marginalization of Palestinian history and identity. Educational materials, public monuments, and even tourism are sometimes used to promote a one-sided historical narrative that diminishes the Palestinian connection to the land.

The destruction and suppression of cultural identity, whether through the Nazi erasure of Jewish culture, Imperial Japan's forced assimilation, or Israel's targeting of Palestinian culture, are powerful tools of domination. By erasing or rewriting the cultural and historical presence of a people, these regimes aim to weaken the spirit of the populations they seek to control, diminishing their sense of identity and belonging. The impact of these actions is profound, as it not only affects the present generation but also seeks to erase the historical memory of a people, leaving future generations disconnected from their cultural roots.

Nazi Erasure of Jewish Culture: Systematic Destruction of Identity and Heritage

AS PART OF ITS GENOCIDAL campaign, the **Nazi regime** not only sought the physical extermination of the Jewish people but also pursued the complete **erasure of Jewish culture and identity**. This cultural annihilation was a crucial element of the Holocaust, as the Nazis aimed to wipe out every trace of Jewish existence from European society. The destruction of **synagogues, cemeteries, art, books,** and other cultural landmarks was deliberate and methodical, designed to obliterate Jewish heritage and ensure that future generations would have no memory of the vibrant Jewish communities that once thrived across Europe.

One of the earliest and most significant events in the **systematic destruction of Jewish culture** was **Kristallnacht**, or the **Night of Broken Glass**, which took place on November 9-10, 1938. During this state-sanctioned pogrom, hundreds of **synagogues** were burned, Jewish businesses were looted and destroyed, and Jewish homes were ransacked. The Nazis shattered the windows of Jewish-owned shops and left the streets covered in broken glass, giving the event its name. Kristallnacht marked a turning point in the Nazi campaign against the Jews, as it was the first large-scale, overt act of violence specifically targeting Jewish culture and property. Synagogues, which had been the centers of Jewish religious and community life, were particularly targeted for destruction, symbolizing the Nazi effort to eradicate not only the people but their spiritual and cultural identity.

The **destruction of Jewish cemeteries** was another key aspect of the Nazis' cultural erasure. Cemeteries, as sacred spaces where generations of Jewish families had been buried, were systematically desecrated. Gravestones were smashed, and in many cases, the stones were repurposed for building materials, further erasing the presence of Jewish history from the landscape. Jewish cemeteries, which had stood for centuries as symbols of continuity and remembrance, were reduced to rubble, depriving the Jewish people of the ability to honor their dead and maintain their historical connections.

The Nazis also targeted **Jewish libraries, schools, and museums**, confiscating and destroying thousands of **books**, **manuscripts**, and **artifacts** that represented Jewish scholarship and cultural achievements. Jewish literature and religious texts, including the **Torah**, were burned in public book burnings, where piles of Jewish and other "un-German" works were set ablaze. These book burnings were intended to signal the cultural cleansing of Jewish intellectualism and history. By destroying Jewish books and artifacts, the Nazis aimed to erase the intellectual contributions of Jewish scholars, writers, and religious figures, ensuring that their influence would no longer be felt in European society.

The looting of **Jewish art collections** was another tactic employed by the Nazis in their quest to obliterate Jewish culture. Jewish families who had amassed significant collections of valuable art, often over generations, saw their homes ransacked and their possessions stolen by the Nazis. In many cases, the most valuable pieces were either destroyed or appropriated by high-ranking Nazi officials and museums. The plunder of Jewish art not only represented a financial loss but also a cultural one, as many of these works had been integral to the Jewish community's artistic heritage.

Jewish cultural landmarks, such as the **Jewish Quarter in Prague** and historic **Jewish ghettos** across Europe, were targeted for demolition. In occupied territories, the Nazis dismantled Jewish neighborhoods, either by forcing Jews into ghettos or by completely razing these areas to make room for new construction. This process of urban destruction and restructuring was aimed at removing any visible trace of Jewish presence in these cities, further contributing to the erasure of Jewish cultural identity.

The **ghettos** themselves, while initially created as places of forced isolation for Jews, became places where Jewish cultural life struggled to survive despite the horrific conditions. In many ghettos, Jews continued to practice their religion, teach their children, and maintain some semblance of cultural continuity through clandestine schools, libraries, and religious ceremonies. However, these efforts were often brutally suppressed, and as the ghettos were liquidated, their residents were deported to concentration and extermination camps where the final act of physical and cultural erasure took place.

The Nazis' ultimate goal was not only to exterminate the Jewish people but to ensure that no trace of their **heritage** remained. By destroying synagogues, looting art, desecrating cemeteries, and burning books, the Nazis sought to obliterate Jewish identity at every level—religious, intellectual, and cultural. This systematic erasure of Jewish culture was part of a broader campaign to create a Europe free of Jewish influence, where the history and contributions of Jewish communities would be forgotten.

Despite the Nazis' efforts, Jewish culture survived, both in the hearts and minds of survivors and through the recovery and preservation of Jewish heritage after the war. Nonetheless, the cultural destruction inflicted by the Nazis left a deep wound that will never fully heal, as countless cultural treasures, historic sites, and lives were irretrievably lost. The Nazi campaign to erase Jewish culture stands as a stark reminder of the dangers of hatred and intolerance, and the need to protect and preserve cultural heritage in the face of oppression.

Imperial Japan's Cultural Suppression: Forced Assimilation in Korea, Taiwan, and China

DURING ITS IMPERIAL expansion in the early 20th century, **Imperial Japan** imposed policies of **cultural suppression** and **forced assimilation** on the territories it occupied, particularly in **Korea, Taiwan,** and parts of **China.** These policies were designed to erase local identities and replace them with Japanese cultural, linguistic, and political norms, under the belief that Japanese culture was inherently superior. This process was not only a means of control but also part of Japan's broader vision of creating a **Greater East Asia Co-Prosperity Sphere**, where Japan would lead and dominate a culturally homogenized region. The goal was clear: to erase the distinct cultural identities of the occupied populations and mold them into loyal subjects of the Japanese Empire.

In **Korea**, which had been under Japanese rule since 1910, the Japanese government implemented a comprehensive program of **cultural erasure**. One of the most prominent aspects of this was the forced adoption of **Japanese names** through the **Soshi-kaimei** policy. Koreans were pressured to abandon their Korean names and adopt Japanese ones, erasing their familial and cultural heritage. This policy was part of a broader attempt to replace Korean identity with Japanese identity, stripping away the language, customs, and traditions that defined Korean culture. **Korean schools** were forced to teach in Japanese, with the curriculum centered on Japanese history and values. Korean history, language, and literature were either banned or severely restricted, and students were taught to view themselves as part of the Japanese Empire, not as Koreans.

The suppression extended to **religious practices** as well. Koreans were pressured to participate in **Shinto rituals**, which were foreign to their religious beliefs and practices. Shintoism, the state religion of Japan, was promoted as a unifying spiritual force for the empire, but in reality, it was used as a tool to enforce Japanese cultural supremacy. Traditional Korean spiritual practices, such as **Buddhism** and **Confucianism**, were sidelined or suppressed, as the Japanese authorities sought to replace them with a state-sanctioned religious framework that reinforced loyalty to Japan.

In **Taiwan**, which came under Japanese rule in 1895 following the **First Sino-Japanese War**, a similar policy of **forced cultural assimilation** was imposed. The Japanese colonial government implemented widespread reforms aimed at integrating Taiwanese society into the Japanese Empire. Like in Korea, **Japanese became the official language** of instruction in schools, and Taiwanese students were required to learn Japanese history and culture. Taiwanese cultural practices, including language, religion, and customs, were marginalized as the colonial government sought to replace them with Japanese norms. Taiwanese were expected to adopt Japanese names, participate in Japanese festivals, and practice Japanese customs, often at the expense of their own cultural traditions.

The Japanese authorities also worked to **reshape Taiwanese society** economically and politically to align it more closely with Japan's interests. Land reforms and industrial policies were introduced to exploit Taiwan's resources for the benefit of Japan's growing empire, further cementing the cultural and economic domination of Japan over the Taiwanese people. Although some Taiwanese elites were co-opted into the colonial administration, the vast majority of the population experienced repression and discrimination under Japanese rule, as their cultural identity was systematically undermined.

In **China**, Japan's policies of cultural suppression were most brutally enforced in the regions it occupied during its wartime expansion in the 1930s and 1940s. The occupation of **Manchuria** in 1931 and the subsequent establishment of the puppet state of **Manchukuo** marked the beginning of Japan's efforts to reshape Chinese society to fit its imperial vision. Japanese officials and settlers were given positions of privilege, while the local Chinese population was subjected to strict control. Schools in Manchuria were required to teach Japanese language and history, and efforts were made to promote **Japanese cultural practices** over traditional Chinese ones.

In the areas of China occupied after the outbreak of the **Second Sino-Japanese War** in 1937, Japanese forces implemented harsh policies of **cultural repression**. In addition to the mass atrocities committed against civilians, such as the infamous **Nanjing Massacre**,

Japan sought to erase Chinese cultural and historical landmarks. Libraries, temples, and other cultural institutions were looted or destroyed, as the Japanese military sought to undermine China's cultural heritage. Chinese citizens were often forced to participate in Japanese rituals or adopt Japanese cultural practices, particularly in the occupied cities and towns where Japanese military rule was strongest.

The broader goal of Japan's cultural suppression in China was to eliminate any resistance to Japanese rule by erasing the cultural identity of the Chinese people. By forcing the population to adopt Japanese customs and norms, the Japanese authorities believed they could create a more compliant and subservient population. However, these efforts only fueled resentment and resistance, as many Chinese viewed Japan's policies as an assault on their national identity.

Throughout all these territories, the suppression of local culture and the forced imposition of Japanese norms were key tools of control for the Japanese Empire. The goal was not just to govern these regions but to transform them into extensions of Japan, where loyalty to the emperor and the Japanese way of life would be paramount. The destruction of local identities was a means of consolidating power, as it aimed to weaken the cultural foundations that could inspire resistance to Japanese rule.

Imperial Japan's policies of cultural suppression left a lasting legacy in these regions, particularly in **Korea** and **Taiwan**, where the scars of forced assimilation still affect national identities today. In the aftermath of Japan's defeat in 1945, both Korea and Taiwan worked to reclaim their cultural heritage and reverse the damage done by decades of cultural erasure. Yet the period of Japanese rule remains a painful chapter in their histories, one defined by the loss of language, traditions, and cultural autonomy at the hands of an imperial power determined to assert its dominance.

Israel's Targeting of Palestinian Culture:

Destruction of Heritage, Renaming Cities, and Historical Revisionism

IN THE CONTEXT OF THE Israeli-Palestinian conflict, the **targeting of Palestinian culture** has been a deeply contentious issue, with many accusing Israel of systematically erasing Palestinian identity through the destruction of historical sites, the renaming of cities, and historical revisionism. These actions, viewed by Palestinians and their advocates as deliberate attempts to diminish or erase their cultural and historical presence in the region, have contributed to tensions and exacerbated feelings of displacement. Through the destruction of important cultural landmarks, the alteration of place names, and the rewriting of historical narratives, the cultural identity of Palestinians has faced significant pressure, further complicating the prospect of peaceful coexistence and reconciliation.

One of the most visible forms of cultural targeting has been the **destruction of Palestinian historical sites**. In both **East Jerusalem** and the **West Bank**, numerous Palestinian homes, mosques, and other culturally significant landmarks have been demolished, often under the justification of security concerns or claims that these structures lacked proper building permits. However, for many Palestinians, these demolitions represent a concerted effort to erase their historical and cultural presence in areas that Israel views as vital to its national identity. **Religious sites**, particularly Muslim and Christian landmarks, have also been affected, with some being destroyed or restricted from use, further deepening the cultural divide between Israelis and Palestinians.

In **East Jerusalem**, the Israeli government's expansion of Jewish settlements and infrastructure has led to the displacement of Palestinians and the destruction of historic neighborhoods. **Silwan**, a predominantly Palestinian neighborhood located near the **Old City of Jerusalem**, has been the site of numerous home demolitions to make way for the expansion of Israeli archaeological projects and tourist attractions. These projects often highlight the ancient Jewish history of the area while downplaying or erasing the Palestinian and Islamic connections to the land, leading to accusations of cultural erasure. The destruction of homes and the displacement of residents in historically significant areas have not only physical but also deep symbolic consequences, as they undermine Palestinian ties to Jerusalem and its heritage.

Another major aspect of this cultural targeting is the **renaming of cities and landmarks**. Throughout Israel and the occupied Palestinian territories, many towns and cities that once had Arabic names have been renamed in **Hebrew** as part of a broader effort to assert Israeli sovereignty over the land. This renaming process often involves replacing centuries-old Arabic names with Hebrew ones, effectively erasing the Palestinian historical and cultural connection to these places. For example, **Jaffa**, historically a Palestinian Arab city, has been merged with the neighboring city of Tel Aviv and is now officially referred to as **Tel Aviv-Yafo**, with the Arabic name taking a secondary place. Similarly, many villages that were depopulated during the **1948 Arab-Israeli War** have had their Arabic names replaced, and their historical significance has been diminished in public discourse.

This practice of renaming places is not just a symbolic act; it reflects a broader effort to reshape the historical narrative of the region, framing it as predominantly Jewish in heritage and downplaying or ignoring the long-standing Palestinian presence. By changing the names of towns, streets, and landmarks, the Israeli government seeks to consolidate its claim to the land and present a narrative that aligns with its national identity. For Palestinians, these name changes represent a loss of cultural memory and a form of historical revisionism that attempts to erase their role in the history of the region.

In addition to the physical destruction of sites and the renaming of places, **historical revisionism** plays a critical role in the targeting of Palestinian culture. Israeli narratives often emphasize the Jewish connection to the land of Israel while downplaying or ignoring the presence of Palestinians and their historical claims. This revisionism can be seen in education, public monuments, and even tourism, where the focus is placed on Jewish history, with little mention of Palestinian contributions or the displacement that occurred during the creation of the state of Israel.

In Israeli **school curricula**, for example, the Palestinian narrative of the **Nakba** (the displacement of hundreds of thousands of Palestinians during the 1948 Arab-Israeli War) is often minimized or excluded, while the focus is placed on the Jewish struggle for independence. This lack of acknowledgment of Palestinian suffering and displacement has been a point of contention, as it perpetuates a one-sided historical narrative that erases the Palestinian experience. Similarly, public monuments and museums often highlight Jewish history and culture while ignoring or downplaying the Palestinian heritage of the region. This form of historical revisionism not only shapes public perception but also contributes to the marginalization of Palestinian identity in the broader historical narrative of the land.

The **tourism industry** in Israel also plays a role in shaping the historical narrative. Many tourist sites focus on Jewish and biblical history, often overlooking or minimizing the Palestinian and Islamic historical significance of the same locations. For example, the **City of David** archaeological site in Jerusalem is promoted as evidence of ancient Jewish presence in the city, but little attention is given to the Palestinian families currently living in the surrounding area or the broader historical context of Arab and Islamic presence in Jerusalem. This selective presentation of history reinforces the perception that the land is predominantly Jewish, marginalizing the rich and diverse cultural history that includes Palestinians.

These actions—the destruction of historical sites, the renaming of cities, and historical revisionism—have profound implications for the **Palestinian cultural identity**. They contribute to a sense of dispossession, as Palestinians feel that their historical and cultural ties to the land are being systematically erased. For many Palestinians, this cultural targeting is not just about physical loss; it represents a deeper existential threat to their identity, heritage, and future in the region.

Israel's targeting of Palestinian culture is part of the broader geopolitical struggle between the two peoples, where control over land, history, and identity plays a central role. While Israel sees these actions as part of its efforts to solidify its presence and sovereignty, Palestinians view them as attempts to erase their historical and cultural legacy. The ongoing destruction of Palestinian cultural landmarks, the renaming of cities, and the revision of history serve as powerful tools in this conflict, shaping the narrative of the land and influencing the future of the region's peoples.

Chapter 8: Propaganda and Dehumanization: Justifying Atrocities Through Manipulation of Public Perception

Throughout history, propaganda has been a powerful tool used by regimes to dehumanize targeted groups, shape public opinion, and justify atrocities. By manipulating narratives, distorting the truth, and promoting ideologies of superiority, regimes have successfully created environments where violence against marginalized populations is not only tolerated but encouraged. In Nazi Germany, Imperial Japan, and modern Israel, propaganda has played a central role in constructing narratives that dehumanize Jews, the Chinese, Koreans, and Palestinians, enabling or excusing the violence and repression carried out against these groups. These tactics of propaganda, combined with dehumanization, create a dangerous cycle where atrocities are justified and even celebrated as necessary for the security or progress of the state.

In **Nazi Germany, propaganda** was essential in creating the public mindset necessary to carry out the Holocaust. Under the guidance of **Joseph Goebbels**, the Nazi Minister of Propaganda, a massive media campaign was launched to demonize Jews and other marginalized groups, portraying them as subhuman threats to the German nation. The Nazis used every available medium—newspapers, radio, films, posters, and children's books—to spread antisemitic ideas and to legitimize the discrimination, persecution, and eventual extermination of Jews. Jews were depicted as parasites, vermin, and dangerous conspirators who were responsible for Germany's economic and social problems. This dehumanizing imagery was designed to strip Jews of their humanity, making it easier for ordinary Germans to accept or participate in the regime's genocidal policies.

One of the most infamous examples of Nazi propaganda was the film **"The Eternal Jew"**, which presented Jews as a racial and biological threat to the Aryan race. The film depicted Jews in grotesque caricatures, comparing them to rats, and suggested that their very existence was a threat to German society. Through this propaganda, the Nazis constructed a narrative where the extermination of Jews became a necessary action to protect the German people. The widespread dissemination of these ideas fostered an environment where violence against Jews, including their segregation into ghettos, deportation to concentration camps, and eventual murder in extermination camps, was seen as justified.

The dehumanization of Jews was not limited to visual propaganda. Nazi speeches and writings reinforced the notion that Jews were inferior, subhuman beings who did not deserve the same rights as Aryan Germans. The **Nuremberg Laws** institutionalized this dehumanization, stripping Jews of their citizenship and legal protections. By systematically reducing Jews to a status below human, the Nazi regime created a moral framework that enabled the Holocaust to unfold with widespread complicity or silence from the German population. The success of Nazi propaganda in dehumanizing Jews shows the terrifying power of narrative framing in enabling genocide.

Similarly, **Imperial Japan** used **propaganda** to justify its brutal conquests in **China, Korea**, and throughout Southeast Asia during World War II. Japanese leaders promoted the idea of racial superiority, portraying Japan as the natural leader of Asia and its empire-building efforts as part of a noble mission to "liberate" Asian countries from Western colonial powers. In reality, Japan's imperial ambitions were driven by a desire for territorial expansion and control of resources, but the propaganda framed these efforts as beneficial to the entire region. The ideology of **Pan-Asianism**, which presented Japan as a benevolent leader of a united Asia, masked the reality of Japan's exploitation and violence in the territories it occupied.

In Japanese propaganda, **Chinese people** were often depicted as backward and inferior, and their subjugation was portrayed as necessary for their "civilization" under Japanese rule. The **Second Sino-Japanese War** saw some of the most extreme examples of dehumanizing propaganda, as the Japanese military sought to justify its atrocities, including the **Nanjing Massacre**, where hundreds of thousands of Chinese civilians were raped and murdered by Japanese soldiers. The Japanese media framed the Chinese as subhuman, reinforcing the idea that their suffering was inconsequential or deserved. This dehumanization made it easier for Japanese soldiers to commit acts of extreme violence without moral restraint, as they had been conditioned to view their victims as less than human.

In occupied **Korea** and **Taiwan**, Japanese propaganda emphasized the need for the local populations to assimilate into Japanese culture, portraying Koreans and Taiwanese as racially inferior but capable of improvement through Japanese rule. This propaganda justified the forced assimilation policies, such as the requirement for Koreans and Taiwanese to adopt Japanese names, speak Japanese, and abandon their cultural practices. By framing these populations as lesser but improvable, Japanese propaganda provided a moral justification for the harsh control and exploitation of these territories.

In the modern context, **Israel's media control and narrative framing** have been similarly scrutinized, particularly in how the **Israeli government** portrays **Palestinians**. While the situation differs from the overt racial superiority claims of Nazi Germany or Imperial Japan, Israeli media and government narratives often depict Palestinians in ways that dehumanize them and justify military actions. The Israeli-Palestinian conflict is heavily influenced by how each side is represented in the media, and Israel has been accused of using propaganda to frame Palestinians as violent aggressors while minimizing the broader context of occupation, displacement, and inequality that fuels the conflict.

Israeli media frequently emphasizes **Palestinian violence**, such as rocket attacks from **Gaza** or individual acts of terror, while downplaying or ignoring the systemic violence faced by Palestinians living under Israeli occupation. This selective framing creates a narrative in which Palestinians are seen primarily as threats, while Israeli military actions, including airstrikes, raids, and blockades, are justified as necessary for self-defense. This portrayal not only dehumanizes Palestinians but also diminishes their grievances, reducing their struggle for rights and statehood to a matter of security concerns for Israel.

The Israeli government and media often highlight acts of Palestinian militancy, such as those carried out by **Hamas**, while ignoring or downplaying the impact of Israeli policies on Palestinian civilians, including home demolitions, settlement expansion, and military checkpoints. This narrative control helps maintain public support for Israeli military actions, as it frames Palestinians as violent and irrational, reinforcing the need for strong security measures. At the same time, it marginalizes the voices of Palestinians who seek peaceful solutions and fuels a cycle of dehumanization that prevents meaningful dialogue or resolution.

The **language used by Israeli politicians** and public figures further contributes to this dehumanization. Inflammatory rhetoric that refers to Palestinians as "terrorists" or "wild animals" fosters a perception of Palestinians as inherently violent and incapable of peace, which reinforces the justification for harsh military responses. This narrative framing has significant consequences, as it not only shapes public opinion within Israel but also influences how international audiences perceive the conflict.

In all three cases—**Nazi Germany**, **Imperial Japan**, and **modern-day Israel**—**propaganda** and **dehumanization** serve as powerful tools for shaping public perception and enabling violence. By constructing narratives that strip targeted groups of their humanity, these regimes create environments where atrocities can be carried out with little resistance or moral objection. Whether through portraying Jews as subhuman parasites, the Chinese as racially inferior, or Palestinians as perpetual threats, propaganda plays a critical role in justifying military actions, repression, and human rights violations. The enduring power of propaganda highlights the dangerous impact of narrative control in conflicts where lives are at stake.

Nazi Propaganda: Dehumanizing Jews and Marginalized Groups to Justify Atrocities

NAZI GERMANY'S USE of **propaganda** was one of the most powerful tools in shaping public opinion, reinforcing racial hierarchies, and justifying the atrocities that would culminate in the **Holocaust**. Under the leadership of **Joseph Goebbels**, the **Minister of Propaganda**, the Nazi regime employed a wide array of media—films, newspapers, radio broadcasts, posters, and even educational materials—to create a narrative that dehumanized **Jews** and other marginalized groups. By stripping these people of their humanity, the Nazis made it easier to justify the violence, persecution, and genocide that followed. This propaganda effort was not only about demonizing Jews but also about creating a cultural environment where extreme cruelty was seen as necessary and even patriotic.

From the early days of the Nazi regime, Jews were depicted as a threat to Germany, both racially and economically. Propaganda portrayed Jews as **parasites** or **vermin**, feeding off the hard work of true Germans and weakening the moral fabric of the nation. **Posters** and **cartoons** in Nazi newspapers like **Der Stürmer** regularly depicted

Jews in grotesque, exaggerated forms—often with large noses, greedy expressions, and claw-like hands. This visual portrayal of Jews as subhuman was crucial in creating a mental image that facilitated widespread acceptance of their mistreatment. It was easier for the public to accept segregation, disenfranchisement, and eventually mass murder when Jews were seen as fundamentally different and inferior.

One of the most infamous propaganda films of the era, **"The Eternal Jew"**, further reinforced these stereotypes. Released in 1940, the film depicted Jews as a race of criminals, physically repulsive and morally corrupt. Through a combination of staged scenes and falsified historical narratives, the film suggested that Jews had infiltrated every level of society, secretly controlling finance, media, and politics to the detriment of the German people. The Jews in the film were often compared to rats—creatures that spread disease and filth. This comparison was deliberate: by portraying Jews as less than human, the Nazis made it easier for the German population to rationalize their eventual extermination. Dehumanization made it possible to perceive the mass murder of millions as a necessary and justified action for the protection of the Aryan race.

The **Nuremberg Laws** of 1935, which institutionalized the racial hierarchy promoted by Nazi propaganda, were a direct result of this campaign of dehumanization. These laws stripped Jews of their citizenship and forbade intermarriage between Jews and non-Jews, codifying the idea that Jews were racially inferior. Nazi propaganda played a central role in the implementation of these laws by convincing the German public that such measures were necessary to "protect" the purity of the Aryan race. This racial ideology, embedded in Nazi propaganda, laid the groundwork for the physical separation of Jews from the rest of the population through the establishment of **ghettos** and, later, concentration camps.

The **Holocaust**, in which six million Jews were systematically murdered, was made possible in large part by the sustained and intense propaganda campaign that depicted Jews as an existential threat. By the time Jews were deported to **concentration camps** like **Auschwitz**, much of the German public had already been conditioned to view them not as fellow human beings, but as dangerous outsiders who needed to be eliminated. Nazi propaganda dehumanized Jews to such an extent that their persecution, imprisonment, and eventual mass murder could be seen as an act of national defense rather than genocide.

While Jews were the primary target of Nazi propaganda, other marginalized groups were similarly dehumanized to justify their persecution. **Romani people**, often referred to as "Gypsies," were depicted as thieves, vagabonds, and social misfits who contributed nothing to society. Like Jews, they were portrayed as racially inferior and a threat to the Aryan race. Disabled individuals, who were part of the Nazis' **eugenics** program, were depicted as a burden on society, their lives deemed unworthy of protection. The disabled were often referred to as "useless eaters," a term used in Nazi propaganda to convince the public that their extermination was necessary to strengthen the nation.

Nazi propaganda also targeted **political opponents**, particularly communists and socialists, by portraying them as subversive elements working to destroy Germany from within. This narrative allowed the regime to justify the arrest, imprisonment, and execution of thousands of political dissidents without public backlash. The use of propaganda to dehumanize and vilify these groups created a social environment where persecution and violence were normalized and seen as vital for the survival of the Nazi state.

The success of Nazi propaganda lay not only in its content but also in its **ubiquity**. The regime controlled all aspects of media and culture, ensuring that Nazi ideals permeated every corner of public life. **Radio broadcasts**, **newsreels**, and **films** continuously reinforced the idea that Jews, Romani people, and other marginalized groups were enemies of the state. Children were indoctrinated through the Nazi educational system and the **Hitler Youth**, where they were taught to view Jews and other groups with contempt. Even scientific discourse was corrupted, as Nazi "racial science" was used to provide a pseudo-scientific justification for the dehumanization of non-Aryans.

This relentless propaganda campaign succeeded in **normalizing atrocities**. By the time the mass deportations and killings began, large segments of the German population had been thoroughly indoctrinated to accept, if not actively participate in, the violence. The dehumanization of Jews and other marginalized groups through Nazi propaganda was central to the functioning of the regime's genocidal machine. Without it, the horrors of the Holocaust and the widespread complicity of the German public would not have been possible. Nazi propaganda demonstrates the terrifying power of media to distort reality, justify violence, and dehumanize entire populations, with catastrophic consequences.

Imperial Japan's War Propaganda: Justifying Conquest and Atrocities Through Racial Superiority

DURING ITS AGGRESSIVE expansion across East Asia in the early 20th century, **Imperial Japan** employed a sophisticated propaganda campaign to justify its military conquests and the atrocities it committed. Central to this propaganda was the notion of **racial superiority**, which portrayed the Japanese as the rightful rulers of Asia and depicted the populations of Korea, China, and Southeast Asia as racially inferior. By framing its imperial ambitions as a mission to liberate Asia from Western colonial powers and bring "civilization" to these regions, Japan masked its true intentions of domination and exploitation. The narrative of racial superiority not only justified Japan's brutal treatment of occupied peoples but also dehumanized them, making it easier for Japanese soldiers and the public to accept or participate in atrocities.

The ideology of **Pan-Asianism** was a key component of Japan's war propaganda. This concept promoted the idea of a unified Asia under Japanese leadership, with Japan as the "elder brother" guiding other Asian nations toward prosperity and independence from Western influence. The creation of the **Greater East Asia Co-Prosperity Sphere** was presented as a noble effort to free Asia from the grip of Western imperialism. However, in reality, this rhetoric masked Japan's imperial ambitions. Japan sought to expand its empire by conquering and exploiting neighboring countries, but its propaganda framed these conquests as acts of liberation and racial solidarity.

To achieve this narrative, Japanese propaganda depicted the populations of **China**, **Korea**, and **Southeast Asia** as backward and in need of Japanese guidance. The **Chinese**, in particular, were often portrayed as weak, corrupt, and incapable of self-governance. These depictions were used to justify Japan's invasion of China and the atrocities that followed, such as the **Nanjing Massacre**. During the massacre, Japanese soldiers raped, tortured, and killed hundreds of thousands of Chinese civilians, yet Japanese propaganda presented the invasion as a necessary action to bring order and civilization to China. The Chinese were dehumanized in Japanese media, which depicted them as inferior and unworthy of the same rights and dignity as the Japanese. This dehumanization made it easier for Japanese soldiers to commit atrocities without moral restraint, as they had been conditioned to view the Chinese as less than human.

Similarly, in **Korea**, Japan's colonial rule (1910–1945) was justified through the lens of racial superiority. Japanese propaganda portrayed Koreans as racially and culturally inferior, incapable of self-rule, and in need of Japanese intervention to modernize and civilize their society. Through forced **assimilation policies**, such as the imposition of the Japanese language and the adoption of Japanese names, Koreans were systematically stripped of their cultural identity. This erasure was framed as a benevolent act of bringing Korea into the modern world, but it was, in fact, an extension of Japan's imperial control. Japanese propaganda reinforced the idea that Koreans, as an inferior race, could only improve under Japanese leadership, justifying the harsh repression and exploitation they endured.

Japanese war propaganda also extended to **Southeast Asia**, where countries like the **Philippines**, **Indonesia**, and **Malaya** were invaded and occupied by Japanese forces during World War II. In these regions, Japanese propaganda emphasized the narrative of "liberation" from Western colonial powers, portraying Japan as a savior freeing the people from European and American domination. However, once these regions were under Japanese control, the populations were subjected to forced labor, resource extraction, and brutal military occupation. Japanese propaganda continued to frame these actions as part of Japan's mission to create a prosperous, united Asia, even as the reality for the occupied populations was one of exploitation and suffering.

One of the most infamous aspects of Japan's racial superiority propaganda was the justification of the **"comfort women"** system. Tens of thousands of women, mostly from Korea, China, and the Philippines, were forced into sexual slavery by the Japanese military. Japanese propaganda downplayed or denied the existence of this system, while simultaneously justifying the exploitation of these women as necessary for the war effort. The dehumanization of these women, many of whom were referred to as little more than disposable commodities, was a direct result of the racial hierarchy promoted by Japanese propaganda. The suffering of these women was rendered invisible by the narrative that they were serving a greater cause in support of Japan's war goals.

Throughout its empire, Japan used **racist propaganda** to create a hierarchy that placed the Japanese at the top and all other Asian peoples beneath them. While promoting the idea of Pan-Asian unity,

Japan simultaneously reinforced the notion that other Asian races were inferior and in need of Japanese guidance. This racial superiority was not only used to justify Japan's military expansion but also to legitimize the atrocities committed during the occupation of these territories. The populations of China, Korea, and Southeast Asia were subjected to mass killings, forced labor, and cultural erasure, all under the guise of Japanese benevolence and racial superiority.

Japanese soldiers were also heavily influenced by this propaganda. In military training and indoctrination, they were taught to view the Chinese and other occupied peoples as inferior and less than human. This dehumanization facilitated the extreme brutality exhibited by Japanese forces during the war, including widespread rape, torture, and mass executions. The narrative of racial superiority allowed soldiers to rationalize their actions, believing that they were carrying out their duty to civilize and uplift lesser races, even as they committed unspeakable atrocities.

The Japanese government also controlled **media and education** to ensure that the public supported the war effort. Newspapers, radio broadcasts, films, and textbooks all reinforced the narrative of Japan's racial superiority and its divine mission to lead Asia. The Japanese public was bombarded with images of heroic soldiers and benevolent leaders, while the suffering of occupied populations was hidden or distorted. This constant barrage of propaganda helped maintain public support for the war, even as it became clear that Japan's expansion was not liberating its neighbors but oppressing them.

The legacy of **Imperial Japan's war propaganda** is one of deep scars across Asia. The narrative of racial superiority used to justify Japan's conquests and atrocities left a lasting impact on the region, particularly in countries like China and Korea, where the memory of Japanese occupation remains a source of pain and anger. The dehumanization of entire populations through propaganda contributed to the brutality of the war, fostering an environment where cruelty and violence were normalized. Imperial Japan's use of propaganda as a tool for justifying conquest and racial superiority serves as a stark reminder of the dangers of unchecked nationalism and the power of narrative manipulation in enabling atrocities.

Israel's Media Control and Narrative Framing: Justifying Military Actions Through the Depiction of Palestinians

IN THE ONGOING ISRAELI-Palestinian conflict, **media control** and **narrative framing** play a crucial role in shaping public perceptions and justifying military actions. The **Israeli government** and sympathetic media outlets have been widely criticized for their portrayal of **Palestinians**, often framing them in ways that dehumanize or criminalize them, thereby justifying the harsh military responses and occupation policies. By controlling the narrative, the Israeli government constructs an image of Palestinians primarily as aggressors or terrorists, while downplaying or ignoring the broader context of occupation, displacement, and inequality that fuels Palestinian resistance. This selective framing shapes both domestic and international opinion, allowing Israel to maintain public support for its military actions and policies in the occupied territories.

One of the most common ways the Israeli media frames Palestinians is through the lens of **security concerns**. The narrative often centers on **Palestinian violence**, such as rocket attacks from **Gaza** or stabbings in Israeli cities, which are highlighted as existential threats to the safety of Israeli citizens. This focus on Palestinian militancy reinforces the image of Palestinians as violent and irrational, justifying Israel's military operations and the use of force. The emphasis on security creates a framework in which Israeli airstrikes, ground incursions, and even the construction of the **separation wall** are portrayed as necessary defensive measures rather than acts of aggression.

By concentrating on incidents of Palestinian violence, Israeli media often **dehumanizes** Palestinians, presenting them as little more than a faceless enemy. News coverage tends to highlight Hamas and other militant groups, framing the entire Palestinian population as complicit in terrorism. This broad-brush portrayal ignores the fact that many Palestinians living in the **West Bank** and **Gaza** are civilians who suffer from the consequences of the conflict without being involved in militant activities. The portrayal of Palestinians as inherently violent reinforces a one-sided narrative that justifies military actions as necessary to "defend" Israel, even when those actions lead to high civilian casualties.

The media narrative also downplays the impact of Israeli policies on Palestinian life. **Settlement expansion, home demolitions, military checkpoints**, and the ongoing **blockade of Gaza** are rarely presented in Israeli media as the root causes of Palestinian frustration and resistance. Instead, Palestinian violence is often framed as unprovoked, disconnected from the broader reality of the Israeli occupation and its consequences for Palestinian society. This selective framing minimizes the role of Israeli actions in fueling the conflict and portrays Palestinians as the sole aggressors, justifying Israel's military responses as necessary for maintaining peace and order.

The construction of the **separation wall** is a particularly prominent example of how media framing has been used to justify Israeli actions. Officially referred to as a "security barrier" by the Israeli government, the wall has been depicted in Israeli media as a critical defense measure to prevent Palestinian terrorist attacks. The narrative focuses on how the wall has reduced suicide bombings and other forms of violence, presenting it as a necessary and effective tool for protecting Israeli lives. However, the media often ignores or downplays the fact that the wall cuts deep into the **West Bank**, separating Palestinian communities from their agricultural land, schools, and medical facilities. The portrayal of the wall as a purely defensive structure omits its role in further entrenching the occupation and limiting Palestinian movement, effectively turning Palestinian grievances into a non-issue in the public discourse.

The portrayal of **Palestinians as terrorists** extends beyond acts of physical violence. Palestinian political movements, including non-violent resistance, are often framed in a negative light, portrayed as illegitimate or radical. This framing delegitimizes Palestinian demands for statehood, independence, and equal rights, while reinforcing the idea that Israel's actions, including military occupation and settlement building, are justified in the name of security. The labeling of Palestinian political leaders as extremists or terrorists helps to undermine efforts to reach diplomatic solutions, as it casts any form of Palestinian resistance as a threat to Israel's existence.

Another tool of narrative control is the **language used by Israeli officials** and sympathetic media outlets. Terms like "terrorists," "rioters," and "incitement" are frequently used to describe Palestinians who protest or resist Israeli policies. By contrast, Israeli military actions are often described in neutral or positive terms, such as "operations," "counter-terrorism," or "defense." This disparity in language creates a moral distinction between Israeli and Palestinian actions, where Israeli violence is framed as legitimate and necessary, while Palestinian resistance is portrayed as criminal or violent. The language of security and defense serves to obscure the disproportionate power dynamics of the conflict, where Israel, as a military and economic power, exercises significant control over Palestinian lives.

The control of **international media narratives** is also an important aspect of Israel's media strategy. Israeli officials frequently engage with foreign journalists and news outlets to ensure that the Israeli perspective on the conflict is prominently featured in global coverage. By framing the conflict as one of **self-defense against terrorism**, Israel gains sympathy from Western audiences, particularly in the United States and Europe, where concerns about terrorism resonate strongly. This international narrative often mirrors the one promoted within Israel, focusing on Palestinian violence while ignoring the systemic issues of occupation, settlement expansion, and human rights abuses. This selective narrative helps to ensure that Israeli actions, even those condemned by international human rights organizations, are seen as justified responses to Palestinian aggression.

In contrast, **Palestinian narratives** often struggle to gain traction in mainstream media. Palestinian voices, especially those advocating for peace and human rights, are often marginalized or overshadowed by the focus on violence and terrorism. The result is a one-dimensional portrayal of Palestinians, where the complexity of their experiences under occupation is largely ignored. This lack of representation contributes to the dehumanization of Palestinians and reinforces the perception that their suffering is either deserved or unimportant in the broader geopolitical context.

Ultimately, Israel's control of media narratives and the framing of Palestinians as violent aggressors serve to maintain public support for military actions and occupation policies. By focusing on security and dehumanizing Palestinians, the Israeli government can justify its use of force and continue its policies of expansion and control. This narrative framing not only influences public opinion within Israel but also shapes how the conflict is perceived internationally, ensuring that Israeli actions are viewed as defensive rather than aggressive. The power of media control in shaping perceptions of the conflict highlights the crucial role that narrative plays in justifying violence and perpetuating cycles of oppression.

Chapter 9: Unlawful Expansion and Occupation: Parallels in the Seizure of Land and Territorial Ambitions

Throughout history, the seizure of land and the forced displacement of populations have been central tactics used by expansionist regimes to assert control over new territories. These acts of **unlawful expansion and occupation** are often justified by ideologies of racial superiority, national security, or historical entitlement. In Nazi Germany, the quest for **Lebensraum** (living space) led to the violent takeover of Eastern Europe, with the goal of creating space for the German population. Similarly, **Imperial Japan's occupation and colonization** of vast areas of Asia was driven by a belief in Japan's racial superiority and the need for resources to support its growing empire. In the modern era, **Israel's illegal settlements** in the **West Bank** and the ongoing occupation of Palestinian territories have drawn parallels to these earlier expansionist strategies, as Israel continues to seize land in violation of international law, justifying its actions through security concerns and historical claims.

The **Nazi concept of Lebensraum** was a core element of Adolf Hitler's ideology, which envisioned the expansion of Germany into Eastern Europe to provide more territory for the growing German population. This idea was rooted in a belief in the racial superiority of the **Aryan race** and the need for Germans to dominate the **inferior Slavic populations** of Eastern Europe. The Nazis framed their expansionist policies as necessary for the survival and prosperity of the German people, arguing that Germany needed more land to sustain its population and secure its future. Under this justification, the Nazis launched aggressive military campaigns to seize territory in **Poland**, **Czechoslovakia**, and the **Soviet Union**, displacing millions of people and committing atrocities in the process.

The occupation of these territories was not only about military control but also about the **ethnic cleansing** of non-German populations. In occupied Poland and the Soviet Union, millions of **Jews**, **Slavs**, and other "undesirables" were either killed or forcibly relocated to make way for German settlers. The Nazis implemented a systematic program of **deportations**, **forced labor**, and **genocide** to rid the newly acquired territories of their native populations. This expansionist policy was not only about gaining land but also about reshaping the demographic makeup of Europe to reflect Nazi racial ideology. The brutality of the Nazi occupation in Eastern Europe left deep scars, as entire communities were wiped out, and millions were displaced or killed in pursuit of German territorial ambitions.

Imperial Japan's occupation and colonization of **Korea**, **China**, and much of Southeast Asia mirrored Nazi Germany's expansionist policies in its own quest for dominance. Japan sought to build an empire that would provide the resources and land needed to support its growing population and military ambitions. The Japanese justified their expansion through the ideology of **Pan-Asianism**, claiming that Japan was liberating Asia from Western colonial powers and uniting the region under Japanese leadership. However, in practice, Japan's expansion was driven by a desire for control and exploitation, as it sought to dominate the region economically and politically.

The occupation of territories such as **Manchuria**, **Korea**, and **Southeast Asia** involved the **seizure of land** and the displacement of local populations. In **Manchuria**, Japan established the puppet state of **Manchukuo**, where Japanese settlers were given preferential treatment and the local Chinese population was subjected to harsh repression. Land was confiscated from Chinese and Manchu farmers and redistributed to Japanese settlers, while local industries and resources were exploited for the benefit of the Japanese Empire. Similarly, in **Korea**, the Japanese colonial administration expropriated land from Korean farmers and forced Koreans to work in Japanese-controlled industries. The occupation was marked by brutal repression, forced labor, and the systematic destruction of local cultures.

Japan's expansion into **Southeast Asia** followed a similar pattern. In **Indonesia, Malaysia,** and the **Philippines**, Japanese forces seized control of territory, displacing local populations and exploiting natural resources for the war effort. The occupation of these territories was accompanied by widespread atrocities, including mass killings, forced labor, and sexual slavery. Japan's occupation was justified through propaganda that framed these actions as part of a grand mission to create a unified and prosperous Asia, but in reality, it was driven by imperial ambition and racial superiority.

In the modern era, **Israel's illegal settlements in the West Bank** and the ongoing occupation of Palestinian territories have drawn widespread condemnation from the international community. These settlements are seen by many as a continuation of expansionist policies aimed at seizing land and displacing the local population, much like the territorial ambitions of Nazi Germany and Imperial Japan. Despite multiple **United Nations resolutions** declaring the settlements illegal under international law, Israel continues to expand its presence in the West Bank, building settlements on land that Palestinians claim as part of a future state.

The justification for these settlements is often framed in terms of **security** and **historical entitlement**, with Israeli leaders arguing that the land in the West Bank is part of the historical homeland of the Jewish people. However, the expansion of settlements has led to the **displacement of Palestinians**, the confiscation of Palestinian land, and the creation of a system of apartheid-like segregation, where Israeli settlers enjoy full legal rights, while Palestinians in the same areas are subject to military rule. This has resulted in a deeply divided society, with Palestinians confined to increasingly isolated enclaves, surrounded by Israeli settlements and military checkpoints.

The Israeli government's continued expansion in the West Bank is often compared to the territorial ambitions of Nazi Germany and Imperial Japan, as it involves the **forcible acquisition of land** and the displacement of an indigenous population. The expansion of settlements is seen by many as part of a broader strategy to **permanently annex** parts of the West Bank and prevent the establishment of a viable Palestinian state. International human rights organizations and the **International Court of Justice** have repeatedly condemned Israel's settlement policies, but the Israeli government has continued to expand its presence in the occupied territories, citing security concerns and historical claims.

The parallels between **Nazi Lebensraum**, **Imperial Japan's colonization**, and **Israel's illegal settlements** lie in the use of military force and ideological justification to seize land and displace populations. In all three cases, the expansion was framed as necessary for the survival or prosperity of the nation, but in reality, it involved the violation of international law and the oppression of local populations. These acts of unlawful expansion and occupation have left deep scars on the affected regions, as the displaced populations continue to struggle for justice and recognition.

The **expansionist policies** of Nazi Germany, Imperial Japan, and modern Israel demonstrate the dangers of unchecked territorial ambitions and the devastating impact of occupation on local populations. Whether justified by racial superiority, national security, or historical entitlement, these acts of **unlawful expansion** have caused immense suffering and continue to shape the political landscape of the regions they affected. The lessons of history highlight the need for international accountability and the protection of the rights of displaced populations in the face of aggressive territorial expansion.

Nazi Lebensraum and Expansion into Eastern Europe: Seizure of Land for the German Population

ONE OF THE MOST CENTRAL and destructive components of **Nazi ideology** was the concept of **Lebensraum**, or "living space." This idea, rooted in a belief in the racial superiority of the **Aryan race**, called for the expansion of German territory into **Eastern Europe** to provide space for the growing German population. Adolf Hitler and the Nazi leadership viewed the conquest of Eastern Europe as essential for Germany's survival and dominance, framing it as both a racial and economic necessity. The implementation of Lebensraum led to the systematic displacement, enslavement, and extermination of millions of people in countries like **Poland**, **Czechoslovakia**, and the **Soviet Union**, as the Nazis sought to transform these lands into territories controlled and populated by Germans.

The concept of Lebensraum was not unique to Nazi Germany; it had roots in earlier German nationalist and imperialist thought. However, under Hitler's regime, it became an official policy with devastating consequences. The Nazis believed that the German people, as the superior race, had the right to expand eastward and seize the fertile lands of Poland and the Soviet Union. These lands would serve as the agricultural backbone of a greater German empire, ensuring food security and economic prosperity for generations of Germans. The people who already lived in these regions—primarily **Slavs**, **Jews**, and other ethnic groups the Nazis considered inferior—were seen as obstacles to be removed through **genocide**, **forced deportation**, or **enslavement**.

The Nazi invasion of **Poland** in 1939 marked the first major step in the implementation of the Lebensraum policy. The invasion, which triggered the outbreak of **World War II**, was followed by the brutal occupation of Poland, during which the Nazis began to **ethnically**

cleanse the region. Polish Jews were segregated into **ghettos**, where they were subjected to starvation, forced labor, and eventual deportation to concentration and extermination camps. Non-Jewish Poles were also targeted, with millions deported or forced into slave labor to make way for German settlers. The Nazis planned to turn Poland into a German colony, where ethnic Germans would live on farms and estates taken from the local population.

As the war progressed, Nazi Germany expanded its Lebensraum campaign into the **Soviet Union** with the launch of **Operation Barbarossa** in 1941. This invasion was one of the largest and most brutal military campaigns in history, with the explicit goal of seizing Soviet territory for German use. The Nazis planned to **exterminate or enslave** millions of Soviet citizens, particularly Slavs and Jews, to create space for German settlers. The vast agricultural lands of the Soviet Union, particularly in **Ukraine**, were seen as key to fulfilling Hitler's vision of a self-sufficient German empire.

The Nazi occupation of the Soviet Union was marked by extreme violence and **war crimes**. Millions of civilians were killed in mass shootings, starvation policies, and forced labor camps. The **Einsatzgruppen**, mobile killing units, followed the German army into Soviet territory, systematically murdering Jews, Roma, and political dissidents. The **Holocaust by bullets** in Eastern Europe saw the execution of millions of Jews in open-air massacres, particularly in **Belarus**, **Ukraine**, and the **Baltic states**. The destruction of entire communities was part of the broader Nazi plan to depopulate Eastern Europe and prepare it for German colonization.

The Nazis' long-term vision for Eastern Europe was outlined in the **Generalplan Ost**, a secret Nazi plan that called for the **mass displacement** and extermination of tens of millions of Slavs to make room for German settlers. According to the plan, up to 50 million people in the Soviet Union and Poland would be killed or forced to leave their homes, while the remaining population would be used as a slave labor force for German settlers. Entire regions were to be "Germanized," with cities and towns renamed, local cultures erased, and German families encouraged to move eastward. This plan reflected the depth of the Nazis' racial ideology, which viewed non-German populations as expendable in the pursuit of German expansion.

The **seizure of land** under the Lebensraum policy was not merely a matter of military conquest; it was also an integral part of the **Holocaust** and the Nazis' genocidal agenda. The ethnic cleansing of Eastern Europe was designed to eliminate any resistance to German domination, while the destruction of Jewish and Slavic populations was framed as necessary to ensure the purity and survival of the Aryan race. The Nazis' actions in Eastern Europe left millions dead and displaced, and the region was devastated by the war and occupation.

In addition to the human cost, the **environmental and economic consequences** of the Nazi occupation were profound. The Nazis looted natural resources, destroyed infrastructure, and devastated agricultural production in the territories they occupied. This destruction further deepened the suffering of the local population, who were left without food, shelter, or basic necessities as the war dragged on.

The policy of Lebensraum was ultimately a catastrophic failure. While the Nazis managed to conquer large portions of Eastern Europe, they were unable to maintain control in the face of fierce resistance from Soviet forces and local partisan movements. The sheer scale of the occupation and the brutality of the Nazi policies fueled resentment and rebellion among the occupied populations, contributing to the eventual defeat of Nazi Germany. However, the legacy of Lebensraum remains one of the most horrifying examples of how expansionist ideologies can lead to mass displacement, genocide, and the destruction of entire regions.

The **Nazi pursuit of Lebensraum** serves as a stark reminder of the dangers of expansionist policies based on racial superiority and the dehumanization of others. The crimes committed in the name of securing land for the German population left a lasting scar on Eastern Europe, and the memory of these atrocities continues to shape the region's history and identity. The mass displacement, destruction, and genocide carried out under the Lebensraum policy stand as one of the most egregious examples of how territorial ambitions can lead to unimaginable human suffering.

Imperial Japan's Occupation and Colonization: The Seizure of Territories Across Asia

IMPERIAL JAPAN'S EXPANSIONIST ambitions in the early 20th century were driven by a desire for **resources**, **land**, and **military dominance** across East and Southeast Asia. Framing its conquests under the guise of the **Greater East Asia Co-Prosperity Sphere**, Japan portrayed itself as the liberator of Asian nations from Western colonial rule. In reality, Japan's occupation and colonization of territories such as **Korea, China, Manchuria, Taiwan**, and parts of **Southeast Asia** were marked by brutal exploitation, forced assimilation, and the systematic repression of local populations. These territories were seized to serve Japan's imperial needs, providing resources, labor, and strategic military advantages as Japan sought to build an empire on par with the Western powers it sought to displace.

Japan's imperial ambitions began to take shape with the colonization of **Taiwan** following the **First Sino-Japanese War** (1894–1895). Taiwan became Japan's first overseas colony, and the Japanese government implemented a series of reforms aimed at integrating Taiwan into the Japanese Empire. The Japanese colonization of Taiwan was characterized by the forced assimilation of the local population, including the imposition of the **Japanese language** in schools, the suppression of traditional Taiwanese culture, and the promotion of Japanese customs. The economy was restructured to benefit Japan, with agricultural and industrial production directed toward supporting Japan's growing war machine. Although some infrastructure improvements were made, these primarily served Japanese interests, and the Taiwanese population faced significant repression and discrimination under Japanese rule.

Following Taiwan, Japan set its sights on **Korea**, annexing the peninsula in **1910** after years of increasing political and military influence. The colonization of Korea was one of the most brutal in Japan's imperial history. The Korean population was subjected to harsh laws, forced labor, and a systematic campaign of **cultural erasure. Japanese became the official language** of instruction, and Koreans were pressured to adopt Japanese names. Traditional Korean customs, religious practices, and cultural expressions were suppressed, with the goal of making Koreans loyal subjects of the Japanese Empire. The Japanese government expropriated large swaths of Korean land, redistributing it to Japanese settlers and using Korean labor to fuel Japan's industrial growth. By the time of World War II, Korea had become a critical resource base for Japan's military campaigns, with many Koreans forced into labor camps or conscripted into the Japanese army.

The invasion and occupation of **Manchuria** in **1931** marked a turning point in Japan's expansionist policies. Japan established the puppet state of **Manchukuo** after invading and seizing control of the region from China. Manchuria, rich in natural resources such as coal, iron, and oil, was vital to Japan's industrial and military ambitions. Japan flooded the region with settlers, displacing the local Chinese population and imposing strict colonial control. Under Japanese rule, Manchuria was transformed into an economic and military hub, with forced labor camps established to exploit the local workforce. The **Kwantung Army**, Japan's military force in Manchuria, used the region as a base to launch further incursions into China, leading to the full-scale invasion of China in **1937**.

The **Second Sino-Japanese War**, which began in 1937, was one of the most devastating conflicts in modern history. Japan's occupation of **China** was marked by extreme brutality, including the infamous **Nanjing Massacre**, where hundreds of thousands of Chinese civilians were raped, tortured, and murdered by Japanese soldiers. Japan's military occupation of China involved the systematic exploitation of Chinese resources, forced labor, and the imposition of harsh colonial policies aimed at consolidating Japanese control. The Japanese justified these actions through propaganda that depicted China as a backward nation in need of Japan's civilizing influence. However, in reality, Japan's occupation was driven by a desire to dominate Asia and secure the raw materials and labor necessary to fuel its imperial ambitions.

In **Southeast Asia**, Japan's expansion accelerated during **World War II** as it sought to displace European colonial powers and secure vital resources like oil, rubber, and tin. Japan's occupation of **Malaya**, **Indonesia**, the **Philippines**, and **Burma** (modern-day Myanmar) was characterized by extreme violence and exploitation. Japanese forces committed numerous atrocities against the local populations, including mass killings, forced labor, and sexual slavery. The local economies were restructured to serve Japan's war effort, with resources extracted to support the Japanese military. Japan portrayed its occupation of Southeast Asia as part of a broader effort to liberate the region from Western imperialism, but in reality, it imposed its own form of harsh colonial rule.

One of the most egregious aspects of Japan's occupation policies was the widespread use of **forced labor**. Millions of civilians and prisoners of war were forced to work in dangerous and inhumane conditions in mines, factories, and infrastructure projects designed to support Japan's war effort. In particular, the construction of the **Burma-Thailand Railway**, known as the **Death Railway**, claimed the lives of thousands of forced laborers, including prisoners of war from

Allied nations. The conditions were brutal, with workers facing malnutrition, disease, and constant abuse from Japanese overseers.

Another horrific aspect of Japan's occupation was the use of **comfort women**, a euphemism for the women, mostly from Korea, China, and the Philippines, who were forced into sexual slavery by the Japanese military. These women were often kidnapped or coerced into working in military brothels, where they were subjected to repeated sexual violence and abuse. The comfort women system was a clear reflection of the dehumanizing policies that underpinned Japan's occupation of Asia, where local populations were exploited for the benefit of the empire and treated as expendable resources.

Despite Japan's propaganda framing its expansion as the creation of a **Greater East Asia Co-Prosperity Sphere**, the reality was one of oppression, exploitation, and widespread human suffering. The occupied populations across Asia experienced brutal military rule, forced assimilation, and the destruction of their cultural and economic systems. Japan's colonial ambitions were driven by a desire for territorial and resource dominance, which left a lasting legacy of trauma and destruction in the regions it occupied.

The defeat of **Imperial Japan** in 1945 brought an end to its occupation and colonization of Asia, but the scars of its imperial rule remain. The countries that suffered under Japanese occupation, particularly **Korea**, **China**, and **Southeast Asia**, continue to grapple with the legacy of Japan's atrocities, and the issue of **wartime reparations** and historical memory remains a source of tension in the region. Japan's occupation and colonization of Asia stand as a stark reminder of the dangers of unchecked imperialism and the devastating human cost of territorial expansion.

Israel's Illegal Settlements in the West Bank: International Condemnation and Parallels to WWII Territorial Ambitions

ISRAEL'S POLICY OF building and expanding **illegal settlements** in the **West Bank** has long been a point of contention in the Israeli-Palestinian conflict. These settlements, which are established on land occupied by Israel since the **1967 Six-Day War**, have been widely condemned by the international community as violations of **international law**, particularly the **Fourth Geneva Convention**. This convention prohibits an occupying power from transferring its civilian population into the territories it occupies, yet Israel has continued to build and expand settlements in the West Bank, displacing Palestinians and seizing their land. The expansion of these settlements mirrors the territorial ambitions seen during **World War II**, where aggressive expansionist policies led to the seizure of land and the displacement of populations under the justification of national security or historical claims.

The **West Bank settlements** began shortly after Israel's occupation of the territory in 1967, with the Israeli government initially presenting them as necessary for security and strategic defense. Over time, these settlements expanded significantly, with more than 600,000 Israeli settlers now living in the West Bank and **East Jerusalem**. The Israeli government justifies these settlements by invoking historical and biblical claims to the land, viewing the West Bank (which it refers to as **Judea and Samaria**) as part of the historical homeland of the Jewish people. However, the reality on the ground is that these settlements have led to the **displacement of Palestinian communities**, the confiscation of Palestinian land, and the creation of an apartheid-like system of segregation, where Israeli settlers enjoy full legal rights while Palestinians in the same area are subjected to military rule.

The **international response** to Israel's settlement expansion has been overwhelmingly negative. Numerous **United Nations resolutions**, including **UN Security Council Resolution 2334**, have condemned the settlements as illegal under international law and a major obstacle to peace. Despite this, Israel has continued to expand its presence in the West Bank, building new settlements and expanding existing ones. The Israeli government, particularly under more right-wing administrations, has actively encouraged settlement growth, offering financial incentives and infrastructure support to settlers. This expansion has drawn comparisons to the territorial ambitions of regimes during **World War II**, where land was seized through military force and populated with the occupying power's citizens, often at the expense of the indigenous population.

The **settlements** are not just isolated housing developments; they are connected by a vast network of **settler-only roads** and heavily fortified by the Israeli military. Palestinians in the West Bank face severe restrictions on movement due to the **military checkpoints**, **barriers**, and the **separation wall** that cuts through Palestinian territory. These measures are justified by Israel as necessary for security, but they also serve to fragment Palestinian communities, making it difficult for Palestinians to access their agricultural land, schools, and medical services. The settlements are strategically located to ensure Israeli control over key areas of the West Bank, making the possibility of a contiguous and viable Palestinian state increasingly remote.

The **displacement of Palestinians** as a result of settlement expansion draws a stark parallel to the territorial ambitions of **Nazi Germany** during World War II, particularly the policy of **Lebensraum**. Just as the Nazis sought to expand eastward into **Eastern Europe** to provide "living space" for the German people, displacing and exterminating the local populations, Israel's settlement policy involves the appropriation of land for its own citizens while displacing the Palestinian population. Although the scale and motivations differ, the fundamental dynamic of land seizure and population displacement remains similar. Both policies are based on a belief in the superiority or historical entitlement of one group over another, with devastating consequences for the affected populations.

The expansion of Israeli settlements also mirrors the actions of **Imperial Japan** during its occupation of **Manchuria** and other parts of Asia. Like Nazi Germany, Japan sought to settle its citizens in conquered territories, displacing local populations and exploiting the land for its own benefit. In the case of Israel, the settlements serve not only to establish a permanent Israeli presence in the West Bank but also to change the demographic and political landscape in a way that makes it increasingly difficult for Palestinians to achieve statehood. The continued expansion of settlements undermines the **two-state solution**, which is widely seen as the most viable path to peace in the region.

In addition to international condemnation, human rights organizations have documented numerous **violations of Palestinian rights** in connection with the settlements. Palestinian homes are often demolished to make way for settlement expansion, and Palestinians are frequently denied building permits, forcing them to live in overcrowded conditions or risk having their homes demolished for being built without permits. Israeli settlers, meanwhile, are allowed to build and expand with government support, often on land confiscated from Palestinians. The **violence and intimidation** faced by Palestinians living near settlements is also a major issue, with settler attacks on Palestinian farmers, homes, and property occurring regularly. These attacks are rarely prosecuted, further reinforcing the sense of impunity for Israeli settlers and the double standard in the application of the law.

The **economic impact** of the settlements is another significant issue. By taking control of key agricultural areas and water resources, Israeli settlers have severely limited Palestinian access to the land and resources necessary for their livelihoods. The settlements have also led to the economic isolation of Palestinian communities, as the presence of settlers and the military infrastructure around them makes it difficult for Palestinians to move freely, trade, or develop their economy. This economic strangulation, combined with the physical fragmentation of the West Bank, has deepened Palestinian poverty and dependence on international aid.

The **international community**, including the **European Union**, the **United Nations**, and numerous human rights organizations, continues to call for an end to settlement expansion and the dismantling of illegal settlements. However, efforts to pressure Israel through diplomatic means have been largely unsuccessful, as Israel maintains strong political and military support from key allies, particularly the **United States**. The U.S. has historically vetoed UN resolutions critical of Israel and has provided billions of dollars in military aid, which enables Israel to continue its settlement policies without fear of significant consequences. This support has emboldened Israel to ignore international law and expand its control over the West Bank, further entrenching the occupation.

The **settlement policy** pursued by Israel in the West Bank reflects a broader strategy of **territorial expansion** and **population displacement** that has been seen in history during World War II. While the context and scale may differ, the fundamental principles of seizing land for the benefit of one population while displacing and oppressing another remain disturbingly similar. The expansion of Israeli settlements not only violates international law but also perpetuates a cycle of violence, instability, and injustice in the region, making the prospect of peace between Israelis and Palestinians ever more elusive.

Chapter 10: War Crimes and International Law: A History of Accountability and Its Failures

The concept of **war crimes** and the mechanisms for holding individuals accountable for such acts have evolved significantly since the end of **World War II**. Following the atrocities committed by **Nazi Germany** and **Imperial Japan**, the international community recognized the need for justice and established the **Nuremberg Trials** and the **Tokyo Trials** to prosecute those responsible for crimes against humanity, genocide, and other war crimes. These landmark trials set a precedent for the **prosecution of war criminals**, emphasizing that even during times of war, certain actions are intolerable and must be punished. However, despite the progress made in international law, the **failure to hold Israel accountable** for alleged war crimes committed in the ongoing Israeli-Palestinian conflict raises troubling questions about the selective application of international justice and the **double standards** that exist in the global community.

The **Nuremberg Trials**, held in the aftermath of World War II, were a pivotal moment in the history of international law. The trials, which took place between **1945 and 1946**, were the first of their kind to prosecute leaders of a defeated regime for **crimes against humanity**. Twenty-four of the highest-ranking officials of the **Third Reich**, including military commanders, government ministers, and Nazi ideologues, were brought before an international tribunal. The charges included **genocide**, **war crimes**, and **crimes against humanity**, with a particular focus on the Holocaust and the mass extermination of Jews,

Romani people, and other marginalized groups. The Nuremberg Trials emphasized the idea that individuals, even heads of state and military leaders, could be held personally accountable for their actions during war.

One of the most significant outcomes of the Nuremberg Trials was the establishment of legal precedents for prosecuting war crimes and crimes against humanity. The trials demonstrated that atrocities committed during wartime would no longer be excused as acts of war or carried out under the orders of a superior. The principle of **"command responsibility"** was established, meaning that military and political leaders could be held accountable for the actions of their subordinates if they knew, or should have known, about the crimes being committed. This principle remains a cornerstone of modern international law and has been applied in subsequent war crimes tribunals.

Following the Nuremberg Trials, the **Tokyo Trials**, also known as the **International Military Tribunal for the Far East**, were convened to prosecute the leaders of **Imperial Japan** for war crimes committed during its expansion across Asia and the Pacific. The trials, held between **1946 and 1948**, focused on crimes such as the **Nanjing Massacre**, the abuse and murder of prisoners of war, and the exploitation of civilian populations in occupied territories. Like the Nuremberg Trials, the Tokyo Trials aimed to hold the highest-ranking officials accountable for their role in orchestrating these atrocities.

The **Tokyo Trials** were notable for addressing crimes such as the forced recruitment of **comfort women**, the widespread use of **forced labor**, and the horrific treatment of prisoners of war. Japanese leaders, including Prime Minister **Hideki Tojo** and military commanders, were found guilty of war crimes and crimes against humanity. Some were sentenced to death, while others received lengthy prison sentences. The trials were not without controversy, however, as many lower-ranking officials and military officers were never prosecuted, and the trials were criticized for being selective in their application of justice, particularly regarding the responsibility of the Japanese emperor.

Despite these limitations, both the Nuremberg and Tokyo Trials represented a significant step forward in the international community's efforts to ensure that war criminals could be held accountable for their actions. These trials laid the groundwork for the establishment of permanent international legal bodies such as the **International Criminal Court (ICC)**, which was created in **2002** to prosecute individuals for genocide, war crimes, and crimes against humanity. The principles of accountability, justice, and individual responsibility established during these post-World War II trials remain central to international law today.

However, when it comes to **Israel's actions in the occupied Palestinian territories**, the international community has been much less consistent in its application of these principles. Despite widespread allegations of **war crimes** and violations of international law, including **indiscriminate bombings**, the **targeting of civilians**, and the ongoing **illegal settlement expansion** in the **West Bank**, Israel has largely escaped accountability. This lack of accountability has been a source of deep frustration for Palestinians and their supporters, who see a double standard in how international law is applied.

The **failure to prosecute Israel** for alleged war crimes is often attributed to **political considerations**. Israel enjoys strong diplomatic and military support from powerful nations, particularly the **United States**, which has used its influence in the **United Nations** to block resolutions critical of Israel's actions. This political protection has shielded Israel from many of the consequences that other nations might face for similar actions. In many cases, investigations into potential war crimes, such as those conducted by the **International Criminal Court**, have been stymied by political pressure, leaving victims of these alleged crimes without a clear path to justice.

Israel's legal immunity has been most glaring during its military operations in **Gaza** and the **West Bank**, where accusations of **disproportionate use of force**, **collective punishment**, and the **targeting of civilian infrastructure** have been well-documented by human rights organizations. For example, the **2014 Gaza War**, known as **Operation Protective Edge**, saw widespread destruction in Gaza, with over 2,000 Palestinians killed, the majority of them civilians. Despite calls for investigations into possible war crimes, no significant legal action was taken against Israeli military leaders or government officials responsible for the operation.

One of the main reasons for the lack of accountability is the **influence of powerful allies**, particularly the **United States**, which has consistently vetoed resolutions at the United Nations that seek to investigate or censure Israel for its actions. Additionally, the United States provides billions of dollars in military aid to Israel each year, further emboldening Israel to act with impunity in its military operations. This political dynamic has created a situation where international law is applied selectively, and Israel has been able to avoid the same level of scrutiny faced by other countries accused of similar crimes.

The **illegal settlement expansion** in the West Bank is another glaring example of how Israel has been shielded from international accountability. Despite the fact that the **settlements** violate international law, as recognized by numerous UN resolutions and the **International Court of Justice**, Israel continues to expand its presence in the occupied territories. The construction of these settlements has resulted in the displacement of thousands of Palestinians, the confiscation of Palestinian land, and the creation of an apartheid-like system where Israeli settlers enjoy full legal rights, while Palestinians are subjected to military rule. Despite these clear violations of international law, there have been no significant legal consequences for Israel.

The **lack of accountability** for Israel's actions has led to growing frustration among those who advocate for Palestinian rights and international justice. The failure to prosecute Israeli leaders for alleged war crimes not only undermines the principles of international law but also perpetuates the cycle of violence and instability in the region. The international community's inability or unwillingness to hold Israel accountable sends a message that certain countries are above the law, eroding the legitimacy of international legal institutions and weakening the global commitment to human rights and justice.

The **contrast between the accountability** faced by Nazi and Japanese leaders after World War II and the **lack of accountability** for Israel's actions today is stark. While the Nuremberg and Tokyo Trials set a precedent for prosecuting war crimes and crimes against humanity, the international community's failure to apply these principles consistently has raised serious questions about the effectiveness and fairness of international law. If the global community is to uphold the ideals of justice and accountability, it must find a way to ensure that all nations, regardless of their political alliances, are held to the same standards.

The Nuremberg Trials: Accountability for Nazi War Criminals

THE **Nuremberg Trials** marked a pivotal moment in international justice, serving as the first major attempt to hold leaders of a regime accountable for **war crimes** and **crimes against humanity**. Held between **1945 and 1946**, these trials prosecuted key officials of **Nazi Germany** for their roles in orchestrating the atrocities of **World War II** and the **Holocaust**. The trials took place in **Nuremberg, Germany**, a symbolic location because it was the site of many Nazi rallies. This event set critical legal precedents, establishing that individuals—even heads of state, military leaders, and government officials—could be personally held accountable for actions that violated the laws of war and humanity.

The Nuremberg Trials were initiated by the **Allied powers**—the United States, the United Kingdom, the Soviet Union, and France—after the defeat of Nazi Germany. These powers formed the **International Military Tribunal (IMT)**, which charged 24 of the highest-ranking Nazi officials with **crimes against peace**, **war crimes**, and **crimes against humanity**. Among those on trial were prominent figures like **Hermann Göring**, head of the Luftwaffe, **Rudolf Hess**, Hitler's deputy, and **Joachim von Ribbentrop**, the Nazi foreign minister. These men were accused of planning and executing a war of aggression, committing atrocities against civilians, and participating in the **systematic extermination of Jews**, Romani people, and other groups targeted by the Nazi regime.

One of the most significant aspects of the Nuremberg Trials was the emphasis on **individual responsibility**. The defense used by many of the accused—that they were simply following orders—was rejected by the tribunal. This rejection established the precedent that individuals could not escape accountability for war crimes by claiming they were acting under orders from superiors. The trials reinforced the idea that military personnel and government officials have a moral and legal duty to refuse unlawful orders. This principle of "**command responsibility**" is now a cornerstone of international law and has been applied in subsequent war crimes trials.

The **charges of crimes against humanity** were groundbreaking. The term was relatively new at the time and was used to describe atrocities committed on a massive scale, particularly the genocide of Jews during the Holocaust. For the first time in history, an international court held individuals accountable for mass murder, enslavement, deportation, and the persecution of civilian populations. The **Holocaust** featured prominently in the trials, with extensive evidence presented of the genocide that resulted in the murder of six million Jews. Survivors of concentration camps testified about the horrors they endured, and the tribunal saw documentation of the **gas chambers**, **mass shootings**, and other methods of extermination used by the Nazis.

The prosecution at Nuremberg was divided into four main categories: **crimes against peace**, which involved planning and waging wars of aggression; **war crimes**, which included violations of the laws and customs of war, such as the murder of prisoners of war and the targeting of civilians; **crimes against humanity**, encompassing the Holocaust and other mass atrocities; and **conspiracy to commit these crimes**, which sought to punish those who helped plan and coordinate Nazi policies. The trials meticulously detailed how the Nazi leadership implemented these crimes, showing how they systematically violated international law and human decency.

The tribunal was not without controversy. Critics argued that the trials represented **"victor's justice,"** with the Allied powers judging the defeated Nazi leaders without applying the same standards to their own wartime conduct. Additionally, some questioned the fairness of applying laws retroactively, as many of the charges, particularly those related to crimes against humanity, were not fully established in international law at the time the crimes were committed. Despite these concerns, the Nuremberg Trials were widely seen as a necessary step in addressing the unprecedented scale of the atrocities committed by the Nazi regime.

The outcomes of the Nuremberg Trials were significant. Of the 24 men initially charged, 12 were sentenced to death, including **Hermann Göring**, who committed suicide the night before his scheduled execution. Others, such as **Albert Speer**, the Nazi minister of armaments, received prison sentences, while a few were acquitted. These sentences demonstrated that high-ranking officials could not escape justice simply because they were in positions of power, and that the international community was committed to holding individuals accountable for violations of international law.

One of the most enduring legacies of the Nuremberg Trials is the establishment of the **principle of accountability in international law**. The trials laid the groundwork for future prosecutions of war crimes, including the creation of permanent international legal bodies such as the **International Criminal Court (ICC)**. The legal principles developed at Nuremberg continue to influence global justice, providing a framework for prosecuting individuals responsible for genocide, war crimes, and crimes against humanity.

In addition to shaping modern international law, the Nuremberg Trials were significant in the process of **coming to terms with the Holocaust**. The trials brought to light the full extent of Nazi atrocities, forcing the world to confront the horrors of the genocide. Survivors' testimonies and the overwhelming evidence presented during the trials ensured that the Holocaust would not be forgotten or denied, and they provided a powerful historical record of the systematic extermination carried out by the Nazi regime.

The **Nuremberg Trials** remain a landmark in the pursuit of international justice. They not only held Nazi leaders accountable for their crimes but also established the enduring principle that individuals who commit atrocities, regardless of their rank or position, must face justice. The trials were a crucial step in the development of a legal framework to address war crimes and crimes against humanity, and they continue to serve as a model for the prosecution of international crimes in the modern era.

Tokyo Trials: Holding Japanese Leaders Accountable for Their War Crimes

THE **Tokyo Trials**, formally known as the **International Military Tribunal for the Far East (IMTFE)**, were held between **1946 and**

1948 to prosecute the leaders of **Imperial Japan** for war crimes committed during **World War II**. Following the defeat of Japan in 1945, the Allied powers sought to hold Japanese military and political leaders accountable for the atrocities committed across **Asia** and the **Pacific**. The Tokyo Trials, much like the **Nuremberg Trials** in Europe, aimed to establish justice by prosecuting those responsible for crimes such as **mass killings**, **forced labor**, **sexual slavery**, and the brutal treatment of civilians and prisoners of war. These trials played a crucial role in shaping international law concerning war crimes and crimes against humanity.

The Tokyo Trials were convened under the authority of **General Douglas MacArthur**, the Supreme Commander for the Allied Powers in Japan, and involved judges and prosecutors from **eleven Allied nations**, including the United States, the Soviet Union, China, the United Kingdom, and Australia. The tribunal indicted 28 high-ranking Japanese officials, including **Prime Minister Hideki Tojo**, military commanders, and government ministers, on charges that included **waging wars of aggression**, **war crimes**, and **crimes against humanity**. The focus of the trials was to address the widespread atrocities that occurred during Japan's expansionist campaigns across **China**, **Korea**, **Southeast Asia**, and the **Pacific islands**.

One of the key charges at the Tokyo Trials was **"crimes against peace,"** which included the planning and execution of aggressive wars. The prosecution argued that Japan's military leadership had deliberately engaged in wars of conquest, violating international treaties and agreements. Japan's invasions of **Manchuria** in 1931, **China** in 1937, and its attacks on **Southeast Asia** and the **Pacific** were presented as evidence of a coordinated plan to dominate the region through military force. The tribunal held that these acts of aggression were part of a larger strategy by the Japanese leadership to expand the empire at the expense of neighboring countries, resulting in untold suffering for millions of civilians and soldiers.

The **atrocities committed during the war** were a central focus of the Tokyo Trials. Japan's military was accused of engaging in mass murder, torture, and other war crimes, particularly in **China**, where the infamous **Nanjing Massacre** took place in 1937. During this event, Japanese forces murdered an estimated **300,000 Chinese civilians and disarmed soldiers** in the city of **Nanjing**. Thousands of women were raped, and the city was looted and destroyed. The prosecution presented overwhelming evidence of the massacre, including survivor testimonies, photographs, and military documents, which detailed the systematic nature of the violence perpetrated by Japanese troops.

Another major aspect of the trials was the prosecution of crimes committed against **prisoners of war (POWs)**. Japanese forces were notorious for their brutal treatment of POWs, especially those captured during the campaigns in **Southeast Asia** and the **Pacific islands**. The construction of the **Burma-Thailand Railway**, also known as the **Death Railway**, became a symbol of Japanese cruelty. Tens of thousands of Allied POWs, along with forced laborers from occupied countries, were subjected to inhumane conditions while building the railway. Many died from malnutrition, disease, and brutal beatings by Japanese guards. The tribunal heard testimony from survivors who described the horrific conditions and the systematic abuse they endured while in Japanese captivity.

One of the most notorious crimes addressed at the Tokyo Trials was the forced recruitment of **comfort women**, a euphemism for the **sexual slavery** of women from occupied countries, primarily **Korea**, **China**, and the **Philippines**. These women were forcibly taken to serve in military brothels, where they were subjected to repeated sexual assault by Japanese soldiers. The tribunal documented the extent of this exploitation, which had been sanctioned by the Japanese military as a means to maintain the morale of its troops. The comfort women system was a clear violation of human rights, and the trials sought to bring justice to the women who had suffered under this horrific practice.

While the Tokyo Trials successfully prosecuted many high-ranking Japanese leaders, they were not without controversy. Some critics argued that the trials represented **victor's justice**, with the Allied powers imposing punishment on the defeated Japanese without addressing their own wartime actions. Others pointed out that the emperor of Japan, **Emperor Hirohito**, was not prosecuted, despite his central role as the symbolic and political leader of Japan during the war. Many historians believe that the decision to exempt Hirohito from prosecution was made to facilitate the post-war reconstruction of Japan and to ensure political stability under the emperor's continued reign. This exemption has been a source of lasting debate and criticism, as some argue that the emperor should have been held accountable for Japan's actions during the war.

The outcomes of the Tokyo Trials resulted in **seven death sentences**, including that of **Hideki Tojo**, who was executed in **1948**, and other senior military officials. Sixteen others were sentenced to life imprisonment, and the remaining defendants received shorter prison terms or were acquitted. While the tribunal brought some measure of justice to the victims of Japan's wartime atrocities, the relatively limited number of prosecutions, as well as the exclusion of many lower-ranking officials and military personnel from trial, led some to question whether the trials fully addressed the scope of Japan's war crimes.

Despite these criticisms, the **Tokyo Trials** were a significant step forward in the development of international law concerning war crimes and crimes against humanity. The trials reinforced the principle that military and political leaders could be held accountable for the actions of their forces and that the excuse of "following orders" would not absolve individuals from responsibility for their crimes. The **command responsibility doctrine**, established during the Nuremberg Trials, was reaffirmed in Tokyo, further solidifying the idea that leaders could be prosecuted for failing to prevent or punish war crimes committed by their subordinates.

The legacy of the Tokyo Trials extends beyond the individual convictions. The trials helped lay the groundwork for the **International Criminal Court (ICC)** and other war crimes tribunals that followed, reinforcing the notion that those who commit atrocities, regardless of their position or power, must face justice. The documentation of Japan's war crimes and the international attention brought to these issues through the trials ensured that the suffering of the victims would not be forgotten and that future generations would learn from these horrors.

The **Tokyo Trials** remain a powerful example of the international community's attempt to address war crimes and bring accountability to the highest levels of leadership. While not without their flaws, the trials served as a critical moment in the pursuit of justice for the millions of people who suffered under Japanese occupation and military aggression. They continue to stand as a reminder of the importance of accountability and the ongoing need for international legal frameworks to address crimes against humanity and war crimes.

Israel's Legal Immunity and the Lack of Accountability: The Failure to Prosecute Alleged War Crimes

IN THE ONGOING ISRAELI-Palestinian conflict, **Israel's legal immunity** from prosecution for alleged **war crimes** has been a contentious issue for decades. Despite numerous accusations from international human rights organizations, the **United Nations**, and Palestinian advocacy groups, Israel has largely avoided legal repercussions for actions taken during its military operations in **Gaza**, the **West Bank**, and **East Jerusalem**. These alleged violations of **international law** include the targeting of civilians, disproportionate use of force, illegal settlements, and the blockade of Gaza. The **international community's** failure to hold Israel accountable for these alleged war crimes raises critical questions about **double standards** in the application of justice and the political factors that allow Israel to act with **impunity**.

One of the key reasons for Israel's legal immunity is the **political protection** it receives from powerful allies, particularly the **United States**. The U.S. has historically been Israel's staunchest supporter, providing both military aid and diplomatic backing. In the **United Nations Security Council**, the United States has repeatedly used its **veto power** to block resolutions that would condemn or sanction Israel for its actions in the Palestinian territories. This protection has effectively shielded Israel from international efforts to investigate or prosecute alleged war crimes, even in the face of widespread condemnation from other countries and international bodies. The **political alliance** between Israel and the United States, driven by shared strategic and ideological interests, has allowed Israel to act with relative impunity, even as its military actions are scrutinized by the global community.

A significant focus of the allegations against Israel is its military operations in **Gaza**, particularly during conflicts such as the **2008-2009 Gaza War (Operation Cast Lead)**, the **2014 Gaza War (Operation Protective Edge)**, and more recent escalations. In these conflicts, **Israeli airstrikes** and **ground operations** have caused thousands of Palestinian civilian casualties and widespread destruction of civilian infrastructure, including homes, schools, and hospitals. Human rights organizations, including **Amnesty International** and **Human Rights Watch**, have accused Israel of **disproportionate use of force** and **indiscriminate targeting** of civilian areas, which they argue constitutes violations of international humanitarian law. Under the **Geneva Conventions**, the targeting of civilians and civilian infrastructure in military operations is prohibited, yet Israel has repeatedly faced these accusations without facing meaningful legal consequences.

Another major issue is the continued expansion of **illegal settlements** in the **West Bank** and **East Jerusalem**. According to international law, including the **Fourth Geneva Convention**, it is illegal for an occupying power to transfer its own civilian population into the territory it occupies. However, Israel has built and continues to expand settlements in Palestinian territories, displacing Palestinian residents and expropriating their land. Despite multiple **United Nations resolutions** condemning the settlements as illegal, Israel has faced no serious international legal action to stop their expansion. The settlement policy has not only been a significant obstacle to peace but also a violation of Palestinian rights, as it undermines their claims to land and disrupts the possibility of establishing a future Palestinian state.

The **blockade of Gaza**, imposed by Israel in 2007 after **Hamas** took control of the strip, has also been widely criticized as a form of **collective punishment** against the Palestinian population. The blockade restricts the movement of goods, including essential supplies such as food, medicine, and construction materials, contributing to a humanitarian crisis in Gaza. Human rights organizations have argued that the blockade violates international law by inflicting suffering on the civilian population, yet Israel continues to impose it with little to no accountability. International bodies such as the **United Nations** and the **International Criminal Court (ICC)** have expressed concerns about the legality of the blockade, but political pressures have prevented any substantial legal action from being taken against Israel.

Israel's actions in the **West Bank**, including the demolition of Palestinian homes, the forced displacement of communities, and the construction of the **separation wall**, have also been the subject of international condemnation. The **International Court of Justice (ICJ)** ruled in 2004 that the construction of the separation wall on Palestinian land was illegal and violated international law. The wall, which Israel claims is necessary for security, cuts through Palestinian territories, effectively annexing large swaths of land and severely restricting the movement of Palestinians. Despite the ICJ ruling and ongoing international pressure, Israel has not dismantled the wall or faced legal repercussions for its construction.

The **International Criminal Court** has made some attempts to investigate Israeli actions in the Palestinian territories, but these efforts have been hampered by **political interference** and **diplomatic pressure**. In 2021, the ICC announced it would investigate alleged war crimes committed by both Israel and Palestinian militant groups during the 2014 Gaza conflict and other military operations. However, Israel, which is not a signatory to the **Rome Statute** (the treaty that established the ICC), has refused to cooperate with the investigation, dismissing the court's jurisdiction over its actions. The U.S. and other key allies have also criticized the ICC's investigation, further complicating efforts to hold Israel accountable through international legal mechanisms.

The failure to prosecute Israel for alleged war crimes has deepened Palestinian frustration and undermined faith in the international justice system. Many Palestinians and their supporters view the international community's reluctance to hold Israel accountable as evidence of **double standards** in how international law is applied. While other countries, particularly those with less political influence, have faced sanctions, prosecutions, or military interventions for alleged war crimes, Israel has largely escaped such consequences. This disparity has led to accusations that powerful nations can act with **impunity**, while weaker states are subject to the full force of international law.

The lack of accountability for Israel's actions has not only perpetuated the cycle of violence in the region but also contributed to the ongoing **humanitarian crisis** faced by Palestinians. With no meaningful consequences for its military operations, settlement expansion, or blockade policies, Israel has continued to impose harsh measures on the Palestinian population, further entrenching the occupation and making a peaceful resolution to the conflict increasingly difficult. The absence of accountability also weakens the credibility of international legal institutions, as they are seen as ineffective or biased when it comes to addressing violations committed by powerful states or their allies.

The **international community's** unwillingness to prosecute Israel for alleged war crimes is a glaring example of the selective application of justice. While the principles of **international law** and **human rights** are frequently invoked, they are not applied consistently, particularly when geopolitical interests are at stake. As long as political alliances and strategic considerations continue to shield Israel from accountability, the prospects for achieving justice for the Palestinian people and resolving the conflict remain slim. If the international community is to uphold the principles of international law and human rights, it must ensure that all nations, regardless of their political influence, are held to the same standards.

Chapter 11: Lessons Not Learned: How History Repeats Despite Post-War Promises

After the horrors of **World War II**, the global community made a solemn vow: **"never again."** The atrocities committed during the war, including the **Holocaust**, the mass murders, and the exploitation of civilian populations, left an indelible mark on human history. The **Nuremberg** and **Tokyo Trials** were meant to set a precedent for **international justice**, ensuring that war crimes and crimes against humanity would be punished and that such acts would never happen again. Yet, despite these efforts, the world has repeatedly failed to prevent similar atrocities from occurring. This failure is starkly illustrated by modern conflicts, including **Israel's actions** in the **Palestinian territories**, where allegations of war crimes and violations of international law continue to mount, with little to no accountability.

In the aftermath of World War II, the **United Nations** and various international bodies were established with the mission of maintaining peace and preventing the repetition of the atrocities seen during the war. The creation of the **Universal Declaration of Human Rights** and the **Geneva Conventions** were designed to safeguard the rights of individuals during times of conflict and occupation. These frameworks were intended to ensure that **war crimes**, **genocide**, and **ethnic cleansing** would be condemned and punished by the international community. The establishment of the **International Criminal Court (ICC)** further strengthened these promises, as it was tasked with prosecuting individuals responsible for the most egregious violations of human rights.

However, these **post-war promises** have not been fulfilled. Despite the legal frameworks in place, the world has witnessed numerous conflicts where similar patterns of **violence**, **occupation**, and **displacement** continue to occur. One of the most glaring examples of this failure is the ongoing situation in the **Israeli-Palestinian conflict**. For decades, **Israel's military actions**, **illegal settlement expansions**, and **blockades** have led to the displacement and suffering of Palestinians, drawing accusations of war crimes from international human rights organizations. The international community has repeatedly condemned these actions, yet Israel has largely escaped accountability, benefitting from **political protection** and diplomatic immunity.

The **repetition of history** is evident in the treatment of the Palestinian population. Much like the occupation and territorial expansion of **Nazi Germany** and **Imperial Japan** during World War II, Israel's policies in the West Bank and Gaza Strip involve the seizure of land, the **displacement of populations**, and the use of **military force** to maintain control over the territories. The ongoing **settlement expansion** in the West Bank mirrors the territorial ambitions seen in past regimes, where land is taken from the indigenous population and repurposed for the occupying power. Just as the world vowed never to allow such actions again after World War II, it now turns a blind eye as Israel continues its policies with little resistance from the international community.

The repeated failures to prevent **modern atrocities** raise serious questions about the effectiveness of international law and the **political will** to enforce it. Israel's military operations, such as the repeated bombardments of **Gaza** and the construction of the **separation wall**, have resulted in widespread destruction and loss of life, yet these actions are often framed as necessary for security and defense. While the international community condemns these actions in words, meaningful action to hold Israel accountable has been lacking. This failure to act undermines the very foundations of the post-war international order, which was built on the principles of human rights and justice for all.

The lessons of **World War II**—that unchecked power leads to **atrocities**, and that **war criminals** must be held accountable—seem to have been forgotten in the case of Israel. The **Nuremberg Trials** established that individuals, regardless of their position, must be prosecuted for war crimes. Yet, Israeli leaders responsible for military operations that result in civilian casualties and the destruction of Palestinian infrastructure face no such consequences. This lack of accountability not only perpetuates the conflict but also sets a dangerous precedent for other nations, suggesting that **political alliances** and **strategic interests** can outweigh justice and human rights.

To prevent the repetition of **war crimes** and to hold Israel accountable, the international community must take concrete steps to **reaffirm its commitment** to the principles established after World War II. First and foremost, **international legal bodies** like the ICC must be empowered to carry out investigations and prosecutions without political interference. Israel's refusal to cooperate with international investigations into alleged war crimes must be met with consequences, including **sanctions** or other diplomatic actions. The protection of human rights cannot be contingent on the political interests of powerful nations.

Secondly, there must be a renewed effort to **enforce international law** in the Israeli-Palestinian conflict. This includes ensuring that **illegal settlements** in the West Bank are dismantled and that Palestinians have access to justice for the abuses they have suffered under occupation. The international community must support

Palestinian efforts to seek redress through international legal channels, ensuring that their rights are recognized and protected.

Finally, the world must acknowledge that the **double standards** applied to Israel are eroding the credibility of international institutions. By turning a blind eye to Israel's actions while holding other nations accountable for similar offenses, the global community undermines the legitimacy of its own legal frameworks. If international law is to have any meaning, it must be applied equally to all nations, regardless of their political alliances or economic power.

The promise of "never again" made after World War II is one that the world cannot afford to break. The failure to hold Israel accountable for its actions in the Palestinian territories is a reminder that the lessons of history have not been learned. If the international community truly seeks to prevent the repetition of war crimes and human rights abuses, it must act decisively to enforce the principles of justice and accountability for all nations, including Israel. Only by upholding these values can we hope to stop the cycle of violence and build a future where human rights are respected, and justice prevails.

Post-War Promises: The Vow of "Never Again" After WWII Atrocities

IN THE AFTERMATH OF **World War II**, the world was confronted with the scale of the atrocities committed by **Nazi Germany** and **Imperial Japan**. The revelations of the **Holocaust**, the **genocide** of millions of Jews and other marginalized groups, the use of **forced labor**, and the mass murder of civilians shocked the global conscience. As the world witnessed the full horror of these acts, there was a collective resolve that such crimes should never be allowed to happen again. The phrase **"never again"** became the rallying cry for a new era of **international law**, **human rights**, and **accountability**, as the global community sought to ensure that war crimes and crimes against humanity would not go unpunished and that future generations would be protected from such atrocities.

The **Nuremberg Trials** and the **Tokyo Trials** were key moments in this effort, as the leaders of Nazi Germany and Imperial Japan were prosecuted for their roles in orchestrating the systematic murder, enslavement, and exploitation of millions of people. These trials set important legal precedents, establishing that **individuals**—even heads of state, military commanders, and government officials—could be held personally accountable for **war crimes**, **genocide**, and **crimes against humanity**. The establishment of the **United Nations (UN)** in 1945, with its charter dedicated to maintaining international peace and preventing conflict, was also a direct response to the horrors of the war. The UN was tasked with ensuring that global cooperation would prevent the kinds of unchecked aggression and human rights violations that had led to World War II.

One of the most significant post-war achievements was the adoption of the **Universal Declaration of Human Rights (UDHR)** in 1948. This document was a landmark in international law, outlining the basic rights and freedoms to which all human beings are entitled, regardless of nationality, race, or religion. The UDHR was meant to serve as a moral and legal framework to protect individuals from the kinds of abuses that had occurred during the war. It enshrined principles such as **freedom from torture**, **freedom from slavery**, and the **right to life**, forming the foundation for future human rights treaties and conventions. The UDHR was the world's way of saying that the dignity and rights of every person should be respected, and that atrocities like the Holocaust must never happen again.

In addition to the UDHR, the **Geneva Conventions** were updated in 1949 to provide greater protection for civilians during times of war. These conventions established rules for the treatment of **prisoners of war**, **wounded soldiers**, and **non-combatants**, and prohibited the targeting of civilians in military operations. The Geneva

Conventions sought to ensure that even during armed conflict, there were limits to the destruction that could be inflicted. These legal frameworks were designed to ensure that those who violated international norms would be held accountable, and that future conflicts would be fought with greater respect for human life and dignity.

The creation of the **International Criminal Court (ICC)** in 2002 was another major step in fulfilling the post-war promise of accountability. The ICC was established as a permanent court to prosecute individuals responsible for **genocide, war crimes**, and **crimes against humanity**, and its creation was meant to close the gaps left by previous ad hoc tribunals. The ICC's existence signaled that the international community was serious about enforcing the principles established after World War II, and that no one, regardless of their position, would be above the law when it came to committing atrocities.

However, despite these legal advancements and the promise of "never again," the post-war world has witnessed repeated instances where these ideals have failed. From the **genocides in Rwanda** and **Bosnia** to the ongoing conflicts in **Syria**, **Yemen**, and the **Israeli-Palestinian conflict**, the world has struggled to prevent and respond to atrocities. In many cases, the international community has been slow to act or has turned a blind eye to violations of human rights and international law. Political interests, economic alliances, and geopolitical considerations have often outweighed the commitment to uphold the principles of justice and accountability.

The failure to fully realize the promise of "never again" is most evident in the **Israeli-Palestinian conflict**, where decades of occupation, military aggression, and human rights violations have gone largely unpunished. Despite numerous **UN resolutions** and calls for accountability, Israel's actions in the **West Bank**, **Gaza**, and **East Jerusalem**—including the expansion of **illegal settlements**, the blockade of Gaza, and repeated military operations—have been met with little more than condemnation. The international community's inability to hold Israel accountable for alleged war crimes mirrors the broader failure to enforce the post-war commitments to justice and human rights.

The **political realities** of the modern world, where powerful nations protect their allies from prosecution and international law is applied selectively, have undermined the vision set forth after World War II. The promise of "never again" was meant to apply universally, yet in practice, it has been weakened by the very forces it sought to transcend. While the frameworks established in the post-war era remain critical tools for promoting human rights and preventing atrocities, their effectiveness depends on the willingness of the international community to enforce them consistently and without bias.

The vow of "never again" after World War II was a commitment to a better, more just world, where the horrors of the past would not be repeated. However, the world's failure to live up to this promise, particularly in the case of Israel and other modern conflicts, serves as a stark reminder that **vows alone** are not enough. Without action, accountability, and the political will to uphold international law, the lessons of World War II risk being forgotten, and the cycle of violence and atrocities will continue to repeat.

Repetition of History: The Failure to Prevent Modern Atrocities and Israel's Actions

DESPITE THE LESSONS learned from **World War II** and the global vow of **"never again,"** history has shown that atrocities continue to occur, often with little to no intervention from the international community. The promise of accountability and the protection of human rights, outlined in documents such as the **Universal**

Declaration of Human Rights and the **Geneva Conventions**, has not prevented the repetition of **war crimes**, **ethnic cleansing**, and **occupation** in various parts of the world. One of the most prominent examples of this failure is the ongoing **Israeli-Palestinian conflict**, where Israel's actions in the **West Bank**, **Gaza**, and **East Jerusalem** continue to raise accusations of **human rights violations** and **war crimes**, yet the international response has been largely ineffective.

The **Israeli-Palestinian conflict** is marked by decades of military occupation, land seizures, and systematic policies that have left Palestinians displaced, oppressed, and deprived of basic human rights. Despite numerous **United Nations resolutions** condemning Israel's actions and calling for the protection of Palestinian rights, Israel's settlement expansion in the **West Bank**, its blockade of **Gaza**, and its military operations have persisted. This mirrors the failure of the international community in the lead-up to World War II, when repeated violations of human rights went unchecked, ultimately culminating in the Holocaust and other atrocities.

One of the most significant failures to prevent modern atrocities can be seen in Israel's **settlement policy** in the West Bank. Under international law, the construction of settlements in occupied territories is considered illegal, as outlined in the **Fourth Geneva Convention**, which prohibits an occupying power from transferring its own civilian population into the territory it occupies. However, Israel has continued to build and expand settlements, displacing Palestinians and confiscating their land. The **Israeli government** justifies these actions through historical and security claims, but the reality is that settlement expansion has created a deeply entrenched system of apartheid-like segregation, where Palestinians live under military rule and are denied basic freedoms. This situation draws troubling parallels to the territorial ambitions of **Nazi Germany**, which also sought to displace local populations and take control of land through force.

Israel's **blockade of Gaza** is another example of the failure to prevent atrocities. Since 2007, the Israeli government has imposed a blockade on Gaza, restricting the movement of people and goods in and out of the territory. The blockade has had a devastating impact on the population, resulting in widespread poverty, food shortages, and a lack of access to medical care and essential supplies. Human rights organizations, including **Amnesty International** and **Human Rights Watch**, have accused Israel of committing **collective punishment**, which is prohibited under international law. The blockade, combined with repeated Israeli military operations in Gaza, has led to the destruction of civilian infrastructure and the deaths of thousands of Palestinians, the majority of whom are civilians. Despite this, the international community has largely failed to intervene, allowing the blockade to continue and deepening the humanitarian crisis.

Israel's military operations, particularly in **Gaza**, have also drawn accusations of **disproportionate use of force** and **targeting of civilians**. During the **2014 Gaza War (Operation Protective Edge)**, Israeli airstrikes and ground operations resulted in the deaths of over 2,000 Palestinians, including many women and children. The **United Nations Human Rights Council** and other international bodies have called for investigations into possible war crimes committed by Israel during the conflict, but these calls have gone largely unanswered. The **International Criminal Court (ICC)** has attempted to open investigations into alleged war crimes in Gaza and the West Bank, but Israel's refusal to cooperate with these investigations, combined with political pressure from its allies, particularly the **United States**, has prevented any significant legal action from being taken.

The lack of accountability for Israel's actions is emblematic of the broader failure to prevent modern atrocities. Just as the world failed to stop the rise of **fascism** and the systematic persecution of Jews, Romani people, and others during World War II, it has failed to stop the **occupation** and **oppression** of Palestinians. The international community's repeated calls for a peaceful resolution to the conflict and its condemnation of Israel's actions have not been backed by meaningful action. This failure to enforce international law, hold Israel accountable for its violations, and protect the rights of Palestinians echoes the mistakes of the past, where human rights violations were ignored or excused in the name of political or strategic interests.

Israel's actions, and the international community's failure to prevent them, also reflect a **double standard** in the application of international law. While other countries have faced **sanctions**, **military intervention**, or prosecution for their involvement in war crimes and human rights violations, Israel has largely escaped such consequences due to its political alliances, particularly with the United States. This unequal application of justice undermines the credibility of the international legal system and allows Israel to act with relative impunity, perpetuating the conflict and the suffering of the Palestinian people.

The repetition of history in the case of Israel's actions in the Palestinian territories is a stark reminder that the world has not learned the lessons of the past. The post-war commitment to **justice**, **accountability**, and **human rights** has been weakened by political considerations, and the promise of "never again" has proven to be empty for the people of Palestine. Until the international community takes concrete steps to hold Israel accountable for its actions and enforce the principles of international law consistently and fairly, the cycle of violence and oppression will continue, and the failures of the past will continue to shape the present.

The world's inability to prevent modern atrocities like those committed in the Israeli-Palestinian conflict demonstrates the urgent need for a renewed commitment to **human rights** and **justice**. The repetition of history is not inevitable, but it requires political will and moral courage to break the cycle. If the international community truly seeks to honor the lessons of World War II, it must act decisively to prevent further atrocities and ensure that all nations, including Israel, are held accountable for their actions. Only by doing so can we hope to stop the repetition of history and build a future where human rights are respected for all people.

Call to Action: Steps to Stop the Repetition of War Crimes and Hold Israel Accountable

THE CONTINUED REPETITION of **war crimes** and **human rights violations**, especially in the **Israeli-Palestinian conflict**, demands urgent and decisive action. The failure of the international community to enforce the principles of **international law** and hold Israel accountable for its actions has led to the deepening of the conflict, the perpetuation of the occupation, and the suffering of millions of Palestinians. If the world is serious about preventing the recurrence of atrocities and stopping the cycle of **impunity**, it must take concrete steps to ensure justice, accountability, and the protection of human rights. The time for symbolic condemnations and empty resolutions has passed; meaningful change requires action at every level.

One of the first steps toward ending the repetition of war crimes is to strengthen and empower the role of the **International Criminal Court (ICC)** and other international legal bodies. The **ICC** has the authority to investigate and prosecute individuals responsible for war crimes, crimes against humanity, and genocide, yet its effectiveness has been limited by political interference and the refusal of certain states, including Israel, to cooperate with its investigations. To ensure that Israel is held accountable for its actions, the international community must support the **ICC's** efforts to investigate alleged war crimes committed in the **West Bank** and **Gaza**, and pressure Israel to comply with international law. Countries that have historically shielded Israel from accountability, particularly the **United States**, must cease blocking efforts to bring justice through international legal mechanisms.

Another crucial step is the **enforcement of existing international laws** and **UN resolutions** regarding Israel's occupation of the Palestinian territories. Multiple **United Nations Security Council resolutions** have declared Israel's **settlements** in the **West Bank** illegal under international law, yet the settlements continue to expand with impunity. The international community must go beyond verbal condemnations and take concrete actions, such as imposing **economic sanctions** or **diplomatic consequences** on Israel until it ceases its settlement expansion and respects international law. The failure to enforce these laws only encourages further violations, erodes the credibility of international institutions, and sets a dangerous precedent for other countries engaged in similar activities.

In addition to legal accountability, there must be a concerted effort to address the **humanitarian crisis** in Gaza and the West Bank. The ongoing **blockade of Gaza** has caused immense suffering for its civilian population, leading to food shortages, a lack of medical supplies, and widespread poverty. International organizations, human rights groups, and governments must put pressure on Israel to lift the blockade and allow the free flow of goods and humanitarian aid into Gaza. The blockade, which has been condemned as **collective punishment**, violates international law and exacerbates the conditions that fuel violence and extremism in the region. The international community must work to ensure that the Palestinian population in Gaza is provided with the basic necessities of life, while also advocating for long-term solutions that address the root causes of the conflict.

A **unified diplomatic approach** is also essential for holding Israel accountable. The fragmentation of international efforts, with different countries pursuing conflicting policies, has weakened the global response to the Israeli-Palestinian conflict. To create a cohesive and effective strategy, major powers and regional actors must come together to form a unified stance on Israel's violations of international law. This would include coordinated actions in the **United Nations**, the **European Union**, and other international forums to ensure that Israel faces diplomatic consequences for its continued occupation and military actions in the Palestinian territories. Countries that provide significant military aid and diplomatic support to Israel must use their leverage to press for changes in Israeli policies, particularly in relation to settlement expansion and the use of disproportionate military force.

The international community must also support and amplify the voices of **Palestinians** advocating for justice, human rights, and peace. Too often, Palestinian narratives are marginalized or overshadowed by the dominant narratives that portray the conflict primarily through the lens of Israeli security concerns. It is essential to recognize the legitimacy of Palestinian grievances and their right to self-determination. The international community should invest in **civil society** efforts, human rights organizations, and legal initiatives led by Palestinians that work toward achieving justice and accountability for the violations they face. By empowering these voices and providing them with platforms for advocacy, the international community can help to shift the focus of the discourse toward a more just and balanced approach.

Finally, there must be a **renewed focus on diplomacy** and a commitment to reviving the peace process in a way that centers **justice** and **accountability**. For decades, attempts to negotiate peace between Israelis and Palestinians have faltered due to the lack of enforcement mechanisms, imbalances in power, and the failure to address the root causes of the conflict, including the occupation. A lasting peace can only be achieved if the fundamental issues of justice and human rights are placed at the forefront of diplomatic efforts. This means holding both sides accountable for violations of international law, but it also means addressing the structural inequalities and injustices that underpin the conflict, particularly Israel's occupation of Palestinian land and the denial of Palestinian statehood.

One of the key principles that must guide the international community's efforts is **equal application of the law**. The perception that Israel is shielded from accountability while other nations are held to different standards has severely undermined the credibility of international law and institutions. To rebuild trust in the global legal system, the same rules must apply to all countries, regardless of their political alliances or strategic importance. Holding Israel accountable for its actions is not only a matter of justice for Palestinians; it is essential for the integrity of the international system itself.

In conclusion, stopping the repetition of war crimes and holding Israel accountable requires a multifaceted and coordinated approach that prioritizes **legal accountability**, **human rights**, and **diplomacy**. The international community must move beyond symbolic condemnations and take meaningful steps to enforce international law, support Palestinian rights, and ensure that Israel faces consequences for its violations. Only through such actions can the cycle of impunity be broken, and a path toward justice and peace in the region be forged. The failure to act will only result in the continuation of the conflict, further human suffering, and the erosion of the principles of justice and accountability that the global community has vowed to uphold.

Conclusion: The Unchecked Repetition of Atrocities and the Imperative for Justice

The patterns of **territorial expansion**, **military occupation**, and **systematic human rights violations** seen in **Nazi Germany** and **Imperial Japan** are disturbingly echoed in **Israel's actions** in the **Palestinian territories** today. From the **illegal settlement expansion** in the **West Bank** to the **blockade of Gaza** and the repeated military operations resulting in **civilian casualties**, the parallels between these historical regimes and Israel's policies are clear. Despite the international community's pledge after **World War II** to prevent the repetition of such atrocities, the global response to Israel's actions has been marked by **inconsistency**, **political expediency**, and a failure to enforce **international law**.

Throughout this exploration, key comparisons have emerged. Israel's **settlement expansion**, like the **Lebensraum policy** of Nazi Germany, involves the displacement of an indigenous population to make way for settlers, justified by historical and security claims. Similarly, Israel's **siege tactics** in Gaza mirror **Imperial Japan's use of starvation and collective punishment**, where civilian populations were deliberately targeted to weaken resistance. The Israeli government's control over **narratives and propaganda**, which frames Palestinians as aggressors and justifies military actions, parallels the ways in which both Nazi Germany and Imperial Japan dehumanized their enemies to justify atrocities.

The **moral and legal imperatives** for addressing these actions are undeniable. The international community has long established frameworks, through the **Geneva Conventions**, **Nuremberg Principles**, and **Universal Declaration of Human Rights**, that explicitly prohibit **war crimes**, **crimes against humanity**, and **illegal occupations**. It is essential that the international community recognize Israel's actions for what they are—**violations of international law**—and hold the responsible parties accountable. This is not only about justice for the **Palestinian people** but about upholding the integrity of the **global legal system**. Allowing Israel's actions to go unpunished undermines the very foundations of **international justice** and sends a dangerous message that **powerful nations** can act with impunity, free from the constraints that apply to others.

The **future implications** of allowing these patterns to continue unchallenged are dire. History has shown that **unchecked aggression**, **dehumanization**, and **impunity** lead to greater atrocities and prolonged conflicts. If the world does not act to ensure justice for Palestinians and hold Israel accountable for its **war crimes**, the consequences will extend far beyond the borders of Israel and Palestine. The erosion of **international law** and the weakening of **global institutions** risk creating a world where violations of human rights are normalized, and the most vulnerable populations are left without recourse.

To prevent these dangers, the international community must take decisive steps to ensure **accountability**. This includes supporting investigations by the **International Criminal Court (ICC)**, enforcing **sanctions** and **diplomatic consequences** for Israel's illegal actions, and providing platforms for **Palestinian voices** advocating for justice and human rights. The world cannot afford to repeat the mistakes of the past, where **political considerations** took precedence over **human rights** and **justice**. The time for action is now, and the future of **global**

peace and **stability** depends on the choices made in response to these ongoing violations.

The parallels between Israel's actions and those of **Nazi Germany** and **Imperial Japan** are undeniable, and they highlight the urgent need for accountability. Without meaningful intervention, the repetition of history will continue, with devastating consequences for both the Palestinian people and the international order. It is only by confronting these violations head-on, and by ensuring justice for the oppressed, that the global community can honor its post-war promises and prevent further atrocities.

Summary of Key Points: Direct Comparisons Between Israel's Actions and Those of Nazi Germany and Imperial Japan

THE ACTIONS OF **Israel** in the **Palestinian territories** bear striking similarities to the **war crimes** and **territorial ambitions** exhibited by **Nazi Germany** and **Imperial Japan** during **World War II**. These historical parallels are not only morally troubling but also demonstrate how **modern atrocities** can mirror the very acts the world swore to prevent after the horrors of the mid-20th century.

One of the most glaring comparisons is the policy of **territorial expansion**. Nazi Germany's **Lebensraum** and Imperial Japan's conquest of East Asia were both driven by the desire to **seize land** and displace indigenous populations. Similarly, Israel's ongoing **settlement expansion** in the **West Bank** follows a pattern of confiscating Palestinian land and displacing its residents to make way for Israeli settlers. This process, condemned as illegal under international law, mirrors the aggressive expansionist policies that sought to permanently alter the demographics of the regions they invaded.

The use of **collective punishment** and **siege tactics** also draws a direct comparison between the regimes. Nazi Germany's harsh retaliations in occupied territories and Imperial Japan's brutal **siege strategies** often targeted entire civilian populations to weaken their resistance. Israel's **blockade of Gaza** has had a similar effect, restricting the flow of food, medicine, and essential supplies to over two million Palestinians, creating severe humanitarian crises. Gaza's blockade serves as a form of **collective punishment**, a tactic that violates international law but remains in place with limited global intervention.

In terms of **military tactics**, the **targeting of civilians** is another disturbing parallel. During World War II, Nazi Germany and Imperial Japan engaged in widespread **civilian bombings** and **massacres** to suppress opposition. Israel's repeated **airstrikes on Gaza** and military operations in the **West Bank** have led to significant civilian casualties, including the destruction of homes, hospitals, and schools. Despite claims of targeting militants, these operations often result in the deaths of innocent civilians, further escalating the humanitarian toll in the region.

The manipulation of **media and propaganda** to dehumanize and justify aggressive actions is yet another parallel. Nazi Germany's and Imperial Japan's wartime propaganda depicted their enemies as inferior or dangerous, justifying their brutal policies. Similarly, Israel's media framing often portrays Palestinians as aggressors or terrorists, downplaying the **occupation** and presenting military actions as necessary for national security. This narrative obscures the reality of the occupation and shifts the blame onto Palestinians, much like how propaganda was used in World War II to rationalize atrocities.

In all these comparisons—**territorial conquest**, **collective punishment**, **targeting of civilians**, and **propaganda**—Israel's actions reflect the dangerous patterns seen in the regimes of Nazi Germany and Imperial Japan. These parallels emphasize the failure to learn from history, as well as the need for **international accountability** to prevent further atrocities from occurring in the modern era. By allowing these patterns to continue unchecked, the world risks repeating the darkest chapters of its past.

Moral and Legal Imperatives: Recognizing Israel's Actions as War Crimes

IT IS ESSENTIAL FOR the **international community** to recognize **Israel's actions** in the **Palestinian territories** as **war crimes**, not only from a legal standpoint but also from a moral perspective. The world, after the atrocities of **World War II**, established a framework of **international law** to ensure that such crimes against humanity would never be repeated. The **Geneva Conventions**, the **Universal Declaration of Human Rights**, and the establishment of the **International Criminal Court (ICC)** were created to protect civilians during conflicts, hold perpetrators accountable, and prevent impunity for egregious violations. However, the failure to apply these principles consistently, particularly in the case of Israel's treatment of Palestinians, has undermined global justice and allowed human rights violations to continue unchecked.

The legal basis for recognizing Israel's actions as **war crimes** is well established under international law. The **Fourth Geneva Convention** explicitly prohibits the transfer of an occupying power's civilian population into the territory it occupies, which applies directly to Israel's ongoing **settlement expansion** in the **West Bank**. The **International Court of Justice (ICJ)** has repeatedly ruled that these settlements are illegal, and yet, despite numerous **United Nations resolutions** condemning the practice, Israel has faced no meaningful legal consequences. The continued expropriation of Palestinian land, the destruction of homes, and the displacement of families violate the core principles of international humanitarian law and must be recognized as **crimes against humanity**.

Moreover, Israel's **military operations** in **Gaza** and the **West Bank**, which have led to high civilian casualties and the destruction of civilian infrastructure, raise serious concerns under the laws of war. **Indiscriminate bombings**, the targeting of schools, hospitals, and homes, and the use of disproportionate force violate the **principle of distinction** and **proportionality**, which are foundational to the law of armed conflict. The **blockade of Gaza**, which severely restricts access to essential goods and services, has been condemned as a form of **collective punishment**, a violation of Article 33 of the **Fourth Geneva Convention**. Yet, these violations persist without significant legal repercussions, perpetuating the suffering of millions of Palestinians.

From a moral perspective, recognizing these actions as war crimes is crucial to uphold the **universal principles of human dignity** and **justice**. After the horrors of **World War II**, the world vowed never to allow the systematic oppression and mass violence against civilian populations to go unpunished. Failing to act on these moral imperatives in the case of Israel's actions in the Palestinian territories undermines the very foundation of international human rights law. By ignoring these violations, the global community sends a dangerous message that political alliances and strategic interests can override the **protection of human life** and **fundamental freedoms**.

There is also a **moral obligation** to recognize the **suffering of the Palestinian people**. For decades, Palestinians have lived under occupation, facing daily violence, displacement, and denial of their basic rights. Their pleas for justice and recognition have often been dismissed or minimized in the international arena. Failing to hold Israel accountable for its actions dehumanizes the Palestinian population and perpetuates their status as victims of an unjust system. It is the duty of the international community to stand against all forms of oppression, regardless of the political complexities involved.

Finally, the **danger of impunity** cannot be overstated. Allowing Israel to continue its actions without legal or moral accountability sets a dangerous precedent for other nations and conflicts. It suggests that **powerful states** or those with strong political alliances are above the law, eroding the **rule of law** and weakening global institutions designed to protect human rights. If the international community fails to recognize Israel's actions as war crimes, it undermines the credibility of international law and leaves the door open for other states to commit similar violations with the expectation that they too will escape consequences.

In conclusion, the **moral and legal imperatives** for recognizing Israel's actions as war crimes are clear. The principles of international law, established to protect civilians and hold violators accountable, must be upheld. Failing to do so not only abandons the Palestinian people in their struggle for justice but also endangers the global commitment to human rights, fairness, and accountability. Recognizing these actions as war crimes is a necessary step toward ending the cycle of violence and ensuring that **justice is served**, no matter how politically complex the situation may be.

Future Implications: The Danger of Unchecked Patterns and the Path to Justice for Palestinians

THE FUTURE IMPLICATIONS of allowing **Israel's actions** in the **Palestinian territories** to continue unchallenged are profound and far-reaching, not only for the **Palestinian people** but for the entire global order based on **international law** and **human rights**. The persistent violations of **human rights**, **war crimes**, and **settlement expansion** threaten to entrench a cycle of **violence**, **injustice**, and **impunity** that could destabilize the region and undermine the credibility of international institutions tasked with maintaining global peace and justice. If the international community continues to ignore or downplay these patterns, it risks not only prolonging the suffering of Palestinians but also encouraging similar behavior by other states in conflicts worldwide.

One of the most immediate dangers of leaving Israel's actions unchecked is the complete **erosion of the possibility for peace**. The continued **settlement expansion** in the **West Bank** and the **forced displacement** of Palestinians from their homes make a viable two-state solution increasingly impossible. As Israeli settlements continue to spread, the prospect of a contiguous and sovereign **Palestinian state** diminishes. This creates a reality of **permanent occupation**, where millions of Palestinians live under military rule, deprived of basic human rights and political representation. The failure to challenge these patterns allows for the **entrenchment of apartheid-like conditions**, where Palestinians are subjected to segregation, restricted movement, and systemic discrimination.

Furthermore, allowing these actions to persist without consequences fuels **radicalization** and **extremism** on both sides of the conflict. The Palestinian population, particularly in **Gaza**, has faced decades of **blockade**, **military assaults**, and **economic deprivation**. The lack of justice and accountability for these actions fosters deep resentment, creating fertile ground for extremism and perpetuating cycles of violence. On the other side, continued impunity for Israeli actions emboldens the most extreme elements within Israeli society, leading to further hardline policies, expansion of settlements, and military aggression. Without a clear path to justice and accountability, the conflict will continue to escalate, making a peaceful resolution ever more distant.

The global ramifications of allowing these patterns to continue unchallenged are also severe. If Israel can engage in **occupation**, **collective punishment**, and **war crimes** without facing legal or diplomatic consequences, it sets a dangerous precedent for other states. It signals that **international law** can be selectively applied and that **powerful nations** or those with influential allies can violate the rules with impunity. This weakens the entire system of international justice, encouraging other nations to disregard **human rights** and **international norms** in their own conflicts. The integrity of institutions like the **United Nations**, the **International Criminal Court**, and the broader system of international law is at stake.

To ensure **justice for Palestinians**, the international community must take decisive and coordinated action. First and foremost, there must be a **firm commitment to holding Israel accountable** for its actions under international law. This includes supporting ongoing investigations by the **International Criminal Court (ICC)** into alleged war crimes committed in the **West Bank** and **Gaza**. The international community, particularly Israel's allies, must cease shielding Israel from accountability and instead prioritize **justice** and **human rights** over political expediency. Sanctions, diplomatic pressure, and other legal mechanisms must be used to halt the expansion of illegal settlements, end the blockade of Gaza, and demand adherence to international humanitarian law.

Additionally, the international community must support efforts to empower **Palestinian civil society** and human rights organizations. Palestinians must be given the platform to advocate for their rights and participate meaningfully in the global conversation about their future. This includes providing support for legal cases, amplifying Palestinian voices in international forums, and ensuring that their experiences and struggles are recognized on the global stage. Palestinians deserve the same protections and avenues for justice that are afforded to other oppressed peoples around the world.

Furthermore, there must be a renewed and genuine commitment to **diplomatic solutions** that focus on **justice** and **equality**. The international community must move beyond symbolic gestures and insist on negotiations that prioritize the rights and freedoms of Palestinians. This includes addressing the core issues of **settlement expansion, the right of return for Palestinian refugees, Jerusalem's**

status, and the **end of the occupation**. Only by tackling these root causes can there be a hope for a lasting peace that respects the rights of both Israelis and Palestinians.

In conclusion, the danger of allowing Israel's actions to go unchallenged is clear: it risks not only deepening the **Israeli-Palestinian conflict** but also undermining the entire international system of **justice** and **human rights**. The future will be shaped by the actions taken—or not taken—today. To ensure justice for Palestinians and to preserve the integrity of international law, the global community must stand firm in its commitment to **accountability, equality**, and **human rights** for all. Only by doing so can the patterns of oppression be broken and a future of peace and justice be realized for the Palestinian people.

Appendix

Relevant Documents: Excerpts from International Law, United Nations Resolutions, and Human Rights Reports Condemning War Crimes

The framework of **international law** and the stance of the **United Nations** provide clear guidelines that define and condemn **war crimes**, **illegal occupations**, and **human rights violations**. Below are key excerpts from **international legal instruments**, **UN resolutions**, and **human rights reports** that establish the legal foundations for addressing **Israel's actions** in the **Palestinian territories** as violations of international law and war crimes.

1. The Fourth Geneva Convention (1949)

Article 49:

"The Occupying Power shall not deport or transfer parts of its own civilian population into the territory it occupies."

This provision is central to the illegality of Israel's **settlement expansion** in the **West Bank**. The **Geneva Convention** explicitly prohibits an occupying power from settling its own population in occupied territories, a practice that Israel continues to engage in, violating this cornerstone of international humanitarian law.

Article 33:

"No protected person may be punished for an offense he or she has not personally committed. Collective penalties and likewise all measures of intimidation or of terrorism are prohibited."

This article condemns the **collective punishment** of civilians, a key issue in Israel's **blockade of Gaza**. The restriction of essential goods and services to Gaza's entire population as a form of punishment constitutes a violation of this principle, as it targets civilians who are not involved in hostilities.

2. United Nations Security Council Resolution 242 (1967)

"Emphasizing the inadmissibility of the acquisition of territory by war and the need to work for a just and lasting peace in which every State in the area can live in security, [the resolution] affirms the necessity for the withdrawal of Israeli armed forces from territories occupied in the recent conflict."

This resolution underscores the principle that territory cannot be acquired through military conquest. Israel's continued occupation of the West Bank and **East Jerusalem**, as well as the expansion of settlements in these areas, directly violates the spirit of **UNSC Resolution 242**, which calls for withdrawal from occupied territories.

3. United Nations Security Council Resolution 2334 (2016)

"Reaffirms that the establishment by Israel of settlements in the Palestinian territory occupied since 1967, including East Jerusalem, has no legal validity and constitutes a flagrant violation under international law... Calls upon Israel to immediately and completely cease all settlement activities in the occupied Palestinian territory."

Resolution 2334 is one of the most explicit condemnations of Israel's settlement activities, labeling them as a "flagrant violation" of international law. It calls for an immediate halt to all settlement expansion, reflecting the international community's consensus on the illegality of Israel's actions in the occupied territories.

4. Rome Statute of the International Criminal Court (1998)

Article 8 – War Crimes:

"For the purpose of this Statute, 'war crimes' means: ... Intentionally directing attacks against the civilian population as such or against individual civilians not taking direct part in hostilities... The transfer, directly or indirectly, by the Occupying Power of parts of its own civilian population into the territory it occupies."

The **Rome Statute**, which established the **International Criminal Court (ICC)**, clearly defines **war crimes**, including the transfer of an occupying power's civilian population into occupied territory (applicable to Israel's settlement policy) and the targeting of civilians in military operations. The Rome Statute provides the legal basis for prosecuting individuals responsible for these crimes, and the ICC has sought to investigate Israel's actions, although political challenges have hindered its progress.

5. International Court of Justice (ICJ) Advisory Opinion (2004) on the Separation Wall

"The Court concludes that the construction of the wall by Israel in the Occupied Palestinian Territory, including in and around East Jerusalem, is contrary to international law... Israel is under an obligation to cease forthwith the works of construction of the wall being built in the Occupied Palestinian Territory, to dismantle forthwith the structure therein situated..."

The **ICJ Advisory Opinion** on Israel's construction of the separation wall in the West Bank is a significant legal ruling. It clearly states that the wall, which cuts deep into Palestinian territory, violates international law and must be dismantled. This opinion also confirms that Israel's actions in the occupied territories, including settlement expansion, constitute breaches of international law.

6. Amnesty International Report on Israel and the Occupied Palestinian Territories (2021)

"Israel's airstrikes on Gaza during May 2021 caused widespread destruction of civilian infrastructure and resulted in numerous civilian casualties, in violation of international humanitarian law... The blockade on Gaza, now in its 15th year, has had a devastating impact on the civilian population, amounting to collective punishment under international law."

This report from **Amnesty International** highlights Israel's continued violations of international humanitarian law, particularly during military operations in Gaza. The use of disproportionate force and the targeting of civilian infrastructure are condemned as war crimes. The **blockade of Gaza** is similarly characterized as a form of **collective punishment**, a violation of the **Fourth Geneva Convention**.

7. **Human Rights Watch Report: "A Threshold Crossed: Israeli Authorities and the Crimes of Apartheid and Persecution" (2021)**

"Israeli authorities are committing crimes against humanity of apartheid and persecution. The findings are based on an overarching Israeli government policy to maintain the domination of Jewish Israelis over Palestinians and grave abuses committed against Palestinians living in the occupied territories, including East Jerusalem."

Human Rights Watch explicitly accuses Israel of committing the crimes of **apartheid** and **persecution** against Palestinians. This report documents the systematic discrimination and domination of Palestinians, further cementing the case for legal accountability under international law for Israel's actions in the occupied territories.

Glossary of Terms

Here is a glossary of key terms used throughout the discussion of **war crimes**, **human rights violations**, and **international law**, particularly in relation to **Israel's actions** in the **Palestinian territories** and comparisons to historical events.

Apartheid

A system of institutionalized racial segregation and discrimination. Under **international law**, apartheid is considered a crime against humanity. It involves policies or practices that systematically oppress and dominate one racial group over another. In the context of **Israel** and the **occupied Palestinian territories**, organizations like **Human Rights Watch** and **Amnesty International** have used the term to describe the **systematic domination** of Palestinians by Israeli authorities.

Ethnic Cleansing

The systematic forced removal of ethnic, racial, or religious groups from a given territory by a more powerful group, often involving violence and terror. Ethnic cleansing aims to homogenize a region by eliminating an undesirable population. While not always recognized as a distinct crime under international law, ethnic cleansing often involves crimes against humanity, including **forced displacement**, **mass killings**, and **genocide**. The forced displacement of **Palestinians** during the creation of **Israel** in 1948 (referred to as the **Nakba**) and through subsequent settlement expansions has drawn comparisons to ethnic cleansing practices.

Collective Punishment

A punitive measure taken against an entire population or group for the actions of individuals or smaller groups within that population. Collective punishment is prohibited under the **Fourth Geneva Convention. Israel's blockade of Gaza**, which restricts access to food, medicine, and essential supplies for over 2 million civilians, has been widely condemned as a form of collective punishment, as it targets the entire civilian population in response to actions taken by **Hamas** or other groups within Gaza.

War Crimes

Serious violations of the laws of war that give rise to individual criminal responsibility. War crimes are defined under the **Geneva Conventions**, the **Rome Statute**, and other instruments of **international law**. Examples include the **targeting of civilians**, **torture**, and the destruction of civilian infrastructure not justified by military necessity. **Israel's military operations** in Gaza, involving the **bombing of civilian homes** and infrastructure, have been accused of constituting war crimes due to the disproportionate use of force and failure to distinguish between combatants and non-combatants.

Genocide

The intentional destruction, in whole or in part, of a national, ethnic, racial, or religious group. Genocide involves acts such as killing members of the group, causing serious bodily or mental harm, inflicting conditions calculated to bring about the group's physical destruction, and forcibly transferring children. While **genocide** is not commonly associated with the Israeli-Palestinian conflict, the term has been invoked in discussions of historic events like the **Holocaust** and **ethnic cleansing** in other global conflicts.

Occupation

The control and governance of a territory by a foreign military power. Under **international law**, an occupation is supposed to be temporary, with the occupying power obligated to maintain the status quo and protect the rights of the occupied population. **Israel's occupation of** the **West Bank**, **East Jerusalem**, and **Gaza** has been criticized for becoming a **de facto annexation**, with ongoing **settlement expansion**, displacement of Palestinians, and the imposition of military rule.

Illegal Settlements

Civilian communities established by an occupying power on territory it controls, in violation of international law. **Israeli settlements** in the West Bank, including **East Jerusalem**, are considered illegal under the **Fourth Geneva Convention**, which prohibits the transfer of an occupying power's civilian population into the territory it occupies. These settlements are seen as a major obstacle to peace and a violation of Palestinian rights, as they involve the appropriation of land and resources.

Proportionality

A principle in the law of armed conflict that requires any military action to be proportionate to the legitimate military objective. Under this principle, attacks should not cause excessive harm to civilians or civilian property relative to the direct military advantage anticipated. **Israel's airstrikes** on civilian areas in Gaza, where the number of civilian casualties far outweighs any potential military gain, have been criticized for violating the principle of proportionality.

Right of Return

The principle that individuals who have been displaced or forced to flee their homes, especially as a result of war, have the right to return to their place of origin. This concept is central to the **Palestinian refugee issue**, with millions of Palestinians and their descendants demanding the right to return to the lands from which they were displaced in 1948 and 1967. Israel opposes this, citing demographic concerns.

Blockade

The prevention of goods, services, and people from entering or leaving a territory, usually enforced by military means. Blockades can be legal under **international law** if they are used in times of war and follow specific guidelines, but they cannot be used to **starve civilians** or impose collective punishment. Israel's blockade of **Gaza**, which has severely restricted access to food, medicine, and other basic necessities, has been widely condemned as illegal, contributing to a humanitarian crisis.

Self-Determination

The right of people to freely determine their political status and pursue their economic, social, and cultural development. This principle is enshrined in **international law** and is central to the **Palestinian struggle for statehood**. Palestinians have long sought recognition of their right to self-determination through the establishment of an independent state within the pre-1967 borders, a demand that has been consistently blocked by Israeli policies and international inaction.

Crimes Against Humanity

Widespread or systematic attacks directed against civilian populations, committed as part of a state or organizational policy. Crimes against humanity include acts such as murder, enslavement, deportation, and persecution. **Human rights organizations** have accused Israel of committing **crimes against humanity** in the context of its military operations, occupation, and settlement policies, particularly when civilians are deliberately targeted or oppressed on a large scale.

This glossary serves as a reference for understanding the legal and moral context in which **Israel's actions** in the **Palestinian territories** are being analyzed and compared to historical **war crimes** and **human rights abuses**. These definitions highlight the gravity of the situation and underscore the **international obligations** to prevent and punish such violations.

www.ingramcontent.com/pod-product-compliance
Lightning Source LLC
Chambersburg PA
CBHW060923140726
47996CB00001B/354